HOLIDAY WISHES™

the Needlecraft™ Shop

PUBLISHER / Donna Robertson
DESIGN DIRECTOR / Fran Rohus
PRODUCTION DIRECTOR / Ange Van Arman

EDITORIAL
Senior Editor / Janet Tipton
Editorial & Graphics Team / Kristine Kirst, Susan Koellner,
Trina Burch, Marianne Telesca, Kim Pierce, Danny Martin

PHOTOGRAPHY
Photographers / Mary Craft, Tammy Cromer-Campbell
Photo Stylist & Coordinator / Ruth Whitaker

PRODUCTION
Book Design & Layout / Debby Keel

PRODUCT DESIGN
Design Coordinator / Brenda Wendling

BUSINESS
C.E.O. / John Robinson
Vice President / Customer Service / Karen Pierce
Vice President / Marketing / Greg Deily
Vice President / M.I.S. / John Trotter

CREDITS
Sincerest thanks to all the designers, manufacturers and professionals whose dedication
has made this book possible. Special thanks to David Norris of
Quebecor Printing Book Group, Kingsport, TN.

Library of Congress Cataloging-in-Publication Data
ISBN: 1-57367-056-1
First Printing: 1996
Library of Congress Catalogue Number: / 95-72041
Published and Distributed by *The Needlecraft Shop, LLC.*
Printed in the United States of America

Introduction

Holidays are out-of-the-ordinary days, scattered across the year like constellations in the night sky. Planning and decorating for these occasions is a never-ending cycle, like the seasons themselves. For many of us, holidays are filled with family and friends, food and merriment. We search high and low for ideas that will give a fresh look or taste to our old family traditions.

Our project designers are a very special group of individuals. Like us, they cook and travel and stitch in preparation for holidays. But being creative souls, craft designers have a talent for pulling fresh ideas – like a magic rabbit pulled from a hat – right out of thin air.

Holiday Wishes is a library of terrific ideas. So, no matter what season it is outside, sit back in your favorite chair with Holiday Wishes, and enjoy the journey ... We know you'll find just the right projects to make all your wishes come true.

ST. NICK & FRIENDS

CHRISTMAS CHARM

HOLIDAY PARTIES

Contents

Fabric photographed with permission of Santee Print Works, Inc., New York, New York

St. Nick & Friends

Catch the spirit
of the season when you
join Santa and his elves at
the North Pole … All Santa's
helpers start early to create magical
Christmas moments that will keep the spirit
of giving alive all year long. So bring
along your needles, canvas
and yarn, put on your elf
cap and slippers,
and get ready to
stitch a bag
full of
fun.

Santa's Elves

Designed by
Sandra Miller Maxfield
and Susie Spier Maxfield

for Santa

SIZE: Box is 5¼" square x 6½" tall, not including bow or elf ring.

MATERIALS: Two sheets of 7-count plastic canvas; 3 yds. red 1½" decorative ribbon; Craft glue or glue gun; Metallic cord (for amount see Color Key); Worsted-weight or plastic canvas yarn (for amounts see Color Key).

CUTTING INSTRUCTIONS:

A: For elves, cut eight according to graph.
B: For gift tag, cut one according to graph.
C: For lid top, cut one 37 x 37 holes (no graph).
D: For lid sides, cut four 8 x 37 holes (no graph).
E: For box sides, cut four 34 x 40 holes (no graph).
F: For box bottom, cut one 34 x 34 holes (no graph).

STITCHING INSTRUCTIONS:

NOTE: F piece is unworked.

1: Using colors indicated and Continental Stitch, work four A pieces according to graph; substituting dk. red for dk. green and dk. green for dk. red, work remaining A pieces according to graph. Using white and Continental Stitch,

work B. Using cord and Slanted Gobelin Stitch over three bars, work C-E pieces in vertical rows according to stitch pattern guide. With matching colors, Overcast unfinished edges of A pieces as indicated on graph and B.

NOTE: Separate black and remaining red into 2-ply or nylon plastic canvas yarn into 1-ply strands.

2: Using 2-ply (or 1-ply) in colors indicated, Backstitch and French Knot, embroider facial detail and letters on A and B pieces as indicated.

3: Alternating contrasting pieces as shown in photo, with lt. pink, Whipstitch A pieces together as indicated, forming elf ring. With cord, Whipstitch C and D pieces together, forming lid; Whipstitch E and F pieces together, forming box. With cord, Overcast unfinished edges of lid and box.

NOTE: Cut two 9¾" and four 7¼" lengths of ribbon.

4: Place 9¾" ribbons across lid as shown; glue ends to inside of lid. Place each 7¼" ribbon across one box side as shown; glue ends to inside and bottom of box. Tie remaining ribbon into a multi-looped bow; glue bow and gift tag to top of lid as shown. Place elf ring over box (see photo); glue to corners. ✧

A – Elf
(cut 8)
19 x 22 holes

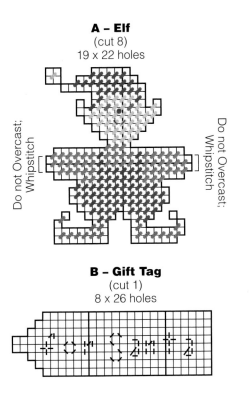

Do not Overcast; Whipstitch

Do not Overcast; Whipstitch

B – Gift Tag
(cut 1)
8 x 26 holes

Lid & Box Stitch Pattern Guide

Continue established pattern up and across each entire piece.

COLOR KEY: Santa's Elves

	Metallic cord			AMOUNT
☐	Gold			110 yds.

	Worsted-weight	Nylon Plus™	Need-loft®	YARN AMOUNT
☐	Dk. Green	#31	#27	18 yds.
☐	Dk. Red	#20	#01	18 yds.
☐	Lt. Pink	#10	#08	10 yds.
☐	Cinnamon	#44	#14	9 yds.
☐	White	#01	#41	6 yds.
■	Black	#02	#00	1 yd.

STITCH KEY:

– Backstitch/Straight Stitch
• French Knot

Jolly Snowmen

Designed by Nancy Marshall

Bring smiles to the faces of your guests when they see Santa's Jolly Snowmen friends through the window.

SIZE: 9¼" x 22".

MATERIALS: One 12" x 18" or larger sheet of stiff 7-count plastic canvas; Four white 9" x 12" sheets of felt; Craft glue or glue gun; Six-strand embroidery floss (for amount see Color Key on page 12); Worsted-weight or plastic canvas yarn (for amounts see Color Key).

CUTTING INSTRUCTIONS:

NOTE: Graphs on page 12.

A: For snowman #1, cut two according to graph.

B: For snowman #2, cut two according to graph.

C: For backings, using one of each A and B piece as a pattern, cut two each from felt ⅛" smaller at all edges.

STITCHING INSTRUCTIONS:

1: Using colors and stitches indicated, work A and B pieces according to graphs; fill in uncoded areas using white and Continental Stitch.

2: Using six strands floss and Backstitch, embroider mouths as indicated on graphs.

3: Alternating A and B pieces, with gray, Whipstitch together as indicated and as shown in photo; with matching colors, Overcast unfinished edges. Glue corresponding C pieces to wrong side of snowmen.✧

Jolly Snowmen

PHOTO ON PAGE 10

COLOR KEY: Jolly Snowmen

	Embroidery floss			**AMOUNT**
■	Red			1 yd.

	Worsted-weight	**Nylon Plus™**	**Need-loft®**	**YARN AMOUNT**
▨	White	#01	#41	45 yds.
▨	Gray	#23	#38	17 yds.
▨	Sail Blue	#04	#35	10 yds.
▨	Yellow	#26	#57	8 yds.
▨	Green	#58	#28	7 yds.
▨	Royal	#09	#32	6 yds.
▨	Pink	#11	#07	1½ yds.
■	Black	#02	#00	1 yd.

STITCH KEY:

— Backstitch/Straight Stitch

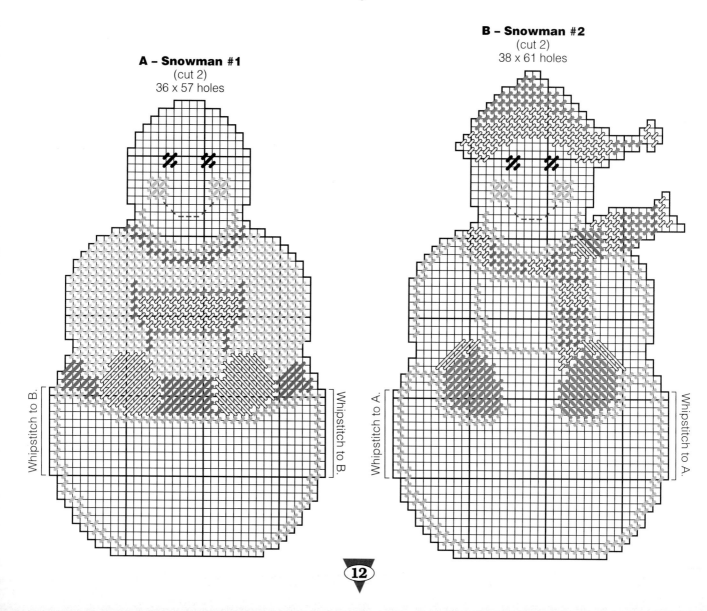

A – Snowman #1
(cut 2)
36 x 57 holes

B – Snowman #2
(cut 2)
38 x 61 holes

Whipstitch to B.

Whipstitch to B.

Whipstitch to A.

Whipstitch to A.

Christmas Stocking

Designed by
Barbara Tipton

Hang this sparkling
stocking with care,
and watch Santa's
helpers fill it with
delightful treats.

Instructions on next page

Christmas Stocking

PHOTO ON PAGE 13

SIZE: 2½" x 8" x 13¼".

MATERIALS: One 12" x 18" or larger sheet of 7-count plastic canvas; One standard-size sheet of 7-count plastic canvas; ¼ yd. red ¼" satin ribbon; 6" red ⅛" satin ribbon; Assorted beads and sequins; Gold craft paint (optional); Two gold 18-mm jingle bells; #9 quilting needle and green sewing thread; Craft glue or glue gun; Six-strand embroidery floss (for amount see Color Key); Pearlized metallic cord (for amount see Color Key); Metallic cord (for amount see Color Key); Heavy (#32) metallic braid or metallic cord (for amounts see Color Key); Raffia straw (for amount see Color Key); Worsted-weight or plastic canvas yarn (for amounts see Color Key).

CUTTING INSTRUCTIONS:

NOTE: Cut one A from standard-size sheet.

A: For front and back, cut two (one for front and one for back) according to graph.

B: For side pieces, cut two 15 x 102 holes (no graph).

STITCHING INSTRUCTIONS:

1: Using colors and stitches indicated, work one A for front according to graph; fill in uncoded areas using red and Continental Stitch. Using white cord and Long Stitch, work remaining A for back on opposite side of canvas according to Back Stitch Pattern Guide; fill in uncoded area using red and Continental Stitch. Using white cord and Long Stitch, work one end of each B piece according to Side Stitch Pattern Guide; overlapping unworked ends of B pieces two holes and working through both thicknesses at overlap area to join, using red and Continental Stitch, work remainder of B pieces, forming side.

2: Using six strands floss, metallic braid and/or metallic cord, raffia and yarn in colors indicated, French Knot and Straight Stitch, embroider detail on front A as indicated on graph.

3: For snowman hatband, thread each end of 6" ribbon from front to back through one ▲ hole as indicated; glue on wrong side to secure. Tie ¼-yd. ribbon into a bow; trim ends. With quilting needle and thread, sew beads to tree and wreath on front A as shown in photo or as desired. Glue sequins and bow to front A as shown or as desired. If desired, place a drop of craft paint in center of each sequin.

4: With matching colors, Whipstitch A and B pieces together according to Stocking Assembly Diagram; with white cord, Overcast unfinished edges.

NOTE: Cut one 4" length of white cord.

5: Thread ends of 4" strand from back to front through upper left corner of Stocking front (see photo); tie one jingle bell to each end as shown. Hang as desired.✧

Side Stitch Pattern Guide

Back Stitch Pattern Guide

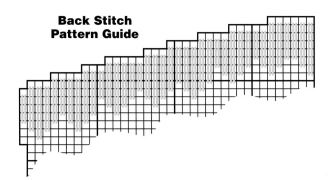

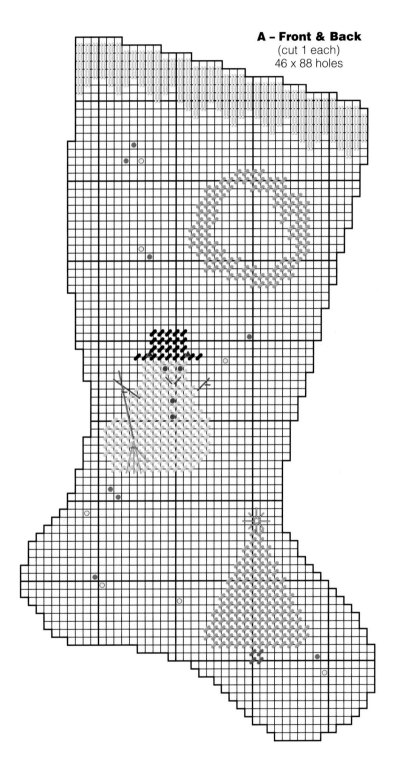

A – Front & Back
(cut 1 each)
46 x 88 holes

COLOR KEY: Christmas Stocking

	Embroidery floss	AMOUNT
■	Black	1/2 yd.

	Pearlized metallic cord	AMOUNT
☐	White	16 yds.

	Metallic cord	AMOUNT
☐	Green	4 1/2 yds.

	Heavy metallic braid or cord	AMOUNT
■	Green	1 yd.
◩	Gold	1 yd.

	Raffia straw	AMOUNT
☐	Gold	1/2 yd.

	Worsted-weight	Nylon Plus™	Need-loft®	YARN AMOUNT
☐	Red	#19	#02	3 1/2 oz.
■	Black	#02	#00	1 yd.
▨	Cinnamon	#44	#14	1/2 yd.

STITCH KEY:

— Backstitch/Straight Stitch
● French Knot
▲ Ribbon Attachment

Stocking Assembly Diagram

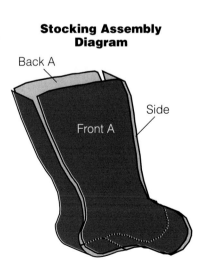

Back A

Side

Front A

Rudolph's Magic

Designed by Diane T. Ray

SIZE: 8" x 12", not including bow or greenery.

MATERIALS: One sheet of 7-count plastic canvas; Musical Blinking Nose with 12-mm red bulb (plays "Rudolph The Red-Nose Reindeer"); One greenery bough (flocking optional); Artificial poinsettia, holly and pine cone/berry sprig or holiday novelties of choice; 1½ yds. red 1½" velveteen ribbon; Sewing needle and red thread; Craft glue or glue gun; Worsted-weight or plastic canvas yarn (for amounts see Color Key on page 18).

CUTTING INSTRUCTIONS:

A: For reindeer, cut one according to graph on page 18.

B: For nose ring, cut one 2 x 20 holes (no graph).

C: For button ring, cut one 3 x 35 holes (no graph).

STITCHING INSTRUCTIONS:

1: Using colors and stitches indicated, work A according to graph; with gray for antlers and with dk. brown, Overcast unfinished edges. Overlapping ends three holes and working through both thicknesses at overlap area to join, using red and Continental Stitch for nose ring and Slanted Gobelin Stitch over narrow width for button ring, work B and C pieces; Overcast unfinished edges.

NOTE: Separate black and dk. brown into 2-ply or nylon plastic canvas yarn into 1-ply strands.

2: Using 2-ply (or 1-ply) in colors indicated and Backstitch, embroider outlines as indicated on graph.

NOTE: Cut six 7" and two 6" lengths of ribbon.

3: For bow, fold each 7" strand of ribbon in half; with sewing needle and thread, tack ends of three folded ribbons to each side of lower cutout on A (see photo). For streamers, tack one end of each 6" ribbon below lower cutout on A (see photo).

4: Insert bulb cover into B according to Nose Assembly Diagram; glue B to A as indicated. Insert music button into C; glue C to A as indicated, inserting wires from front to back through lower cutout. Insert nose light bulb into bulb cover; glue to secure.

5: Tie or glue adornments to greenery bough as shown or as desired. Glue pinecone/berry sprig to A as shown. Glue reindeer assembly to greenery; hang as desired. ✧

Nose Assembly Diagram

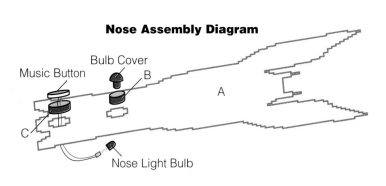

Music Button
Bulb Cover
B
A
C
Nose Light Bulb

Surprise Santa with a Rudolph wall hanging complete with a festive music button.

Rudolph's Magic

INSTRUCTIONS ON PAGE 16

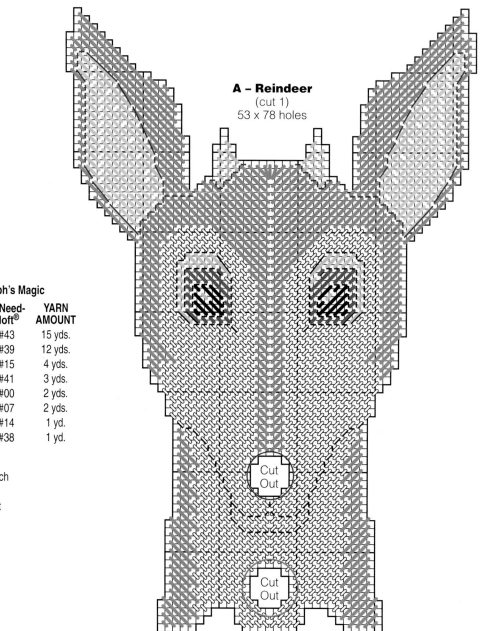

A – Reindeer
(cut 1)
53 x 78 holes

COLOR KEY: Rudolph's Magic

	Worsted-weight	Nylon Plus™	Need-loft®	YARN AMOUNT
	Camel	#34	#43	15 yds.
	Eggshell	#24	#39	12 yds.
	Dk. Brown	#36	#15	4 yds.
	White	#01	#41	3 yds.
	Black	#02	#00	2 yds.
	Pink	#11	#07	2 yds.
	Cinnamon	#44	#14	1 yd.
	Gray	#23	#38	1 yd.

STITCH KEY:

— Backstitch/Straight Stitch
O Nose Ring Placement
O Button Ring Placement

Cut Out

Cut Out

Christmas Pals

Designed by Stephen E. Reedy

Instructions on next page

Christmas Pals

PHOTO ON PAGE 19

SIZE: Each Ornament is about 2½" x 4½".

MATERIALS: One sheet of 7-count plastic canvas; Worsted-weight or plastic canvas yarn (for amounts see Color Key).

CUTTING INSTRUCTIONS:

A: For Santa front, cut one according to graph.

B: For Santa back, cut one according to graph.

C: For Mrs. Claus front, cut one according to graph.

D: For Mrs. Claus back, cut one according to graph.

E: For caroler front, cut one according to graph.

F: For caroler back, cut one according to graph.

G: For elf front, cut one according to graph.

H: For elf back, cut one according to graph.

I: For soldier front, cut one according to graph.

J: For soldier back, cut one according to graph.

STITCHING INSTRUCTIONS:

1: Using colors and stitches indicated, work A-

J pieces according to graphs.

2: Using flesh and French Knot, embroider noses on A, C, E, G and I pieces as indicated on graphs.

NOTE: For remaining embroidery, separate 1¾ yds. of black, ⅓ yd. of red and watermelon into 2-ply or nylon plastic canvas yarn into 1-ply strands.

3: Using 2-ply (or 1-ply) in colors indicated, Backstitch, French Knot and Straight Stitch, embroider facial and clothing detail and book outline on A-G, I and J pieces as indicated.

4: Holding corresponding pieces wrong sides together, with matching colors as shown in photo, Whipstitch together.

NOTE: Cut one 3" length of white.

5: For Santa's hat pom-pom, tie a double knot in the center of 3" strand. To attach the pom-pom and to secure and hide the ends of 3" strand, thread ends into a needle; insert needle between canvas pieces at tip of hat and bring out at opposite canvas edge. Trim ends of 3" strand close to canvas.

6: Use as desired.✧

A – Santa Front
(cut 1)
13 x 29 holes

B – Santa Back
(cut 1)
13 x 29 holes

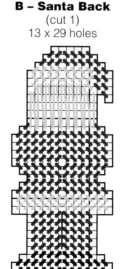

COLOR KEY: Christmas Pals

	Worsted-weight	Nylon Plus™	Need-loft®	YARN AMOUNT
■ Red		#19	#02	19½ yds.
■ Black		#02	#00	8½ yds.
■ Dk. Green		#31	#27	8 yds.
☐ White		#01	#41	8 yds.
■ Cinnamon		#44	#14	7 yds.
☐ Flesh		#14	#56	6½ yds.
▨ Yellow		#26	#57	5 yds.
■ Royal		#09	#32	3 yds.
☐ Gray		#23	#38	2½ yds.
☐ Gold		#27	#17	2 yds.
■ Camel		#34	#43	1 yd.
■ Watermelon		#54	#55	1 yd.

STITCH KEY:

— Backstitch/Straight Stitch

● French Knot

C – Mrs. Claus Front
(cut 1)
19 x 28 holes

D – Mrs. Claus Back
(cut 1)
19 x 28 holes

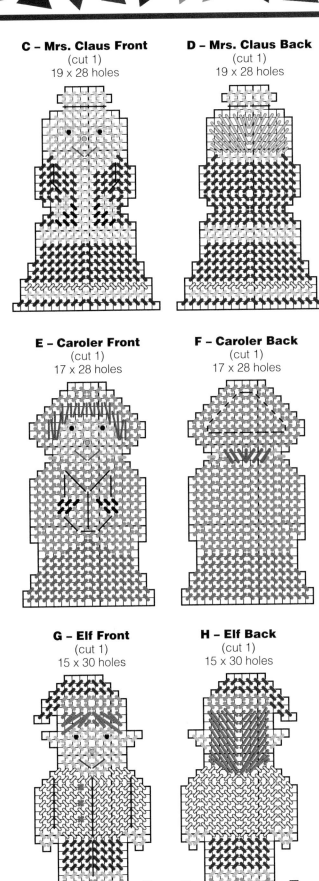

E – Caroler Front
(cut 1)
17 x 28 holes

F – Caroler Back
(cut 1)
17 x 28 holes

G – Elf Front
(cut 1)
15 x 30 holes

H – Elf Back
(cut 1)
15 x 30 holes

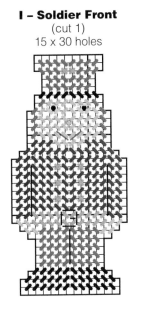

I – Soldier Front
(cut 1)
15 x 30 holes

J – Soldier Back
(cut 1)
15 x 30 holes

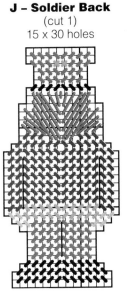

Santa Hanger

Designed by Michele Wilcox

SIZE: 5½" x 10½".

MATERIALS: One sheet of 7-count plastic canvas; #3 pearl cotton or six-strand embroidery floss (for amounts see Color Key); Worsted-weight or plastic canvas yarn (for amounts see Color Key).

CUTTING INSTRUCTIONS:

A: For Santa, cut one according to graph.

STITCHING INSTRUCTIONS:

1: Using colors and stitches indicated, work A according to graph; with matching colors, Overcast unfinished edges.

2: Using pearl cotton or six strands floss and yarn in colors indicated, Backstitch, French Knot and Straight Stitch, embroider hat outline and facial detail as indicated on graph.

3: Hang as desired.✧

A – Santa
(cut 1)
36 x 69 holes

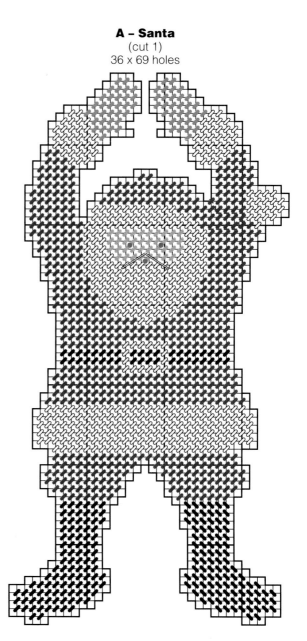

COLOR KEY: Santa Hanger

#3 pearl cotton or floss			AMOUNT
■ Black			½ yd.
■ Blue			½ yd.
■ Red			¼ yd.

	Worsted-weight	Nylon Plus™	Need-loft®	YARN AMOUNT
■	Red	#19	#02	18 yds.
▨	Eggshell	#24	#39	12 yds.
■	Black	#02	#00	6 yds.
▨	Dk. Green	#31	#27	3 yds.
▨	Flesh	#14	#56	1 yd.
▨	Yellow	#26	#57	½ yd.

STITCH KEY:

— Backstitch/Straight Stitch
• French Knot

Accent a cabinet or hang this playful St. Nick in a spot where he's sure to be a part of all the yuletide fun.

Frosty Box

Designed by Michele Wilcox

SIZE: 3¼" x 5¼" x 7½" tall.

MATERIALS: One sheet of 7-count plastic canvas; #3 pearl cotton or six-strand embroidery floss (for amount see Color Key); Worsted-weight or plastic canvas yarn (for amounts see Color Key).

CUTTING INSTRUCTIONS:

A: For front, cut one according to graph.

B: For sides, cut two 17 x 21 holes (no graph).

C: For back, cut one 17 x 34 holes (no graph).

D: For bottom, cut one 21 x 34 holes (no graph).

STITCHING INSTRUCTIONS:

1: Using colors and stitches indicated, work A-D pieces according to graph and stitch pattern guides.

2: Using pearl cotton or six strands floss and yarn in colors indicated, French Knot and Straight Stitch, embroider facial detail and holly berries on A as indicated on graph.

3: With white, Whipstitch A-D pieces together as indicated and according to Box Assembly Diagram. With cinnamon for broom handle and with matching colors, Overcast unfinished edges. ✧

COLOR KEY: Frosty Box

#3 pearl cotton or floss			AMOUNT
◼ Black			1 yd.

Worsted-weight	Nylon Plus™	Need-loft®	YARN AMOUNT
◻ White	#01	#41	45 yds.
◻ Sea Green	#37	#53	2½ yds.
◼ Black	#02	#00	2 yds.
◻ Camel	#34	#43	2 yds.
◼ Cinnamon	#44	#14	2 yds.
◼ Forest	#32	#29	2 yds.
◼ Red	#19	#02	2 yds.
◻ Tangerine	#15	#11	2 yds.

STITCH KEY:

— Backstitch/Straight Stitch

● French Knot

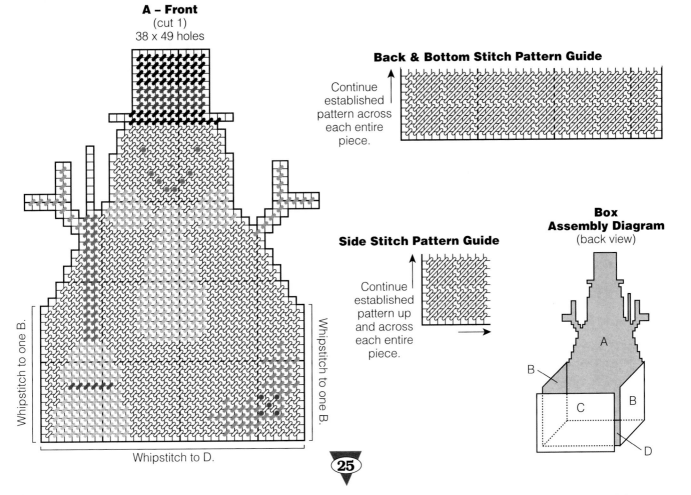

A – Front
(cut 1)
38 x 49 holes

Whipstitch to one B.

Whipstitch to one B.

Whipstitch to D.

Back & Bottom Stitch Pattern Guide

Continue established pattern across each entire piece.

Side Stitch Pattern Guide

Continue established pattern up and across each entire piece.

Box Assembly Diagram
(back view)

A

B

B

C

D

Spread Christmas cheer when you invite these robust figures of Santa and helper to your next party.

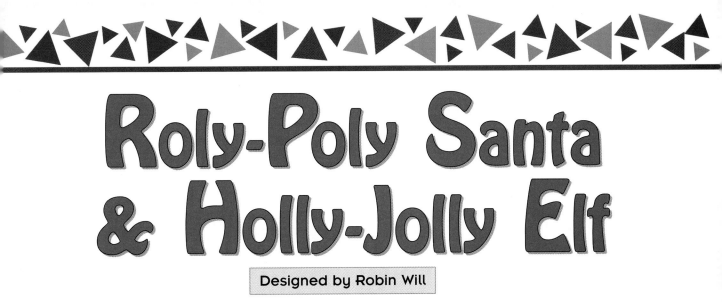

Roly-Poly Santa & Holly-Jolly Elf

Designed by Robin Will

SIZE: Each is about 4¾" x 6" x 12".

MATERIALS: Seven sheets of 7-count plastic canvas; One pink and one red 5-mm pom-pom; One white ½" pom-pom; 10 gold 5-mm jingle bells; Brown and white wool doll hair; 3 yds. gold ⅛" ribbon; ¼ yd. green ⅛" satin ribbon; 2½" square piece each of red and green felt; Polyester fiberfill; One cup aquarium gravel or other weight; Craft glue or glue gun; Metallic cord (for amount see Color Key on page 28); Worsted-weight or plastic canvas yarn (for amounts see Color Key).

CUTTING INSTRUCTIONS:

NOTE: Graphs on pages 28 & 29.

A: For heads, cut two according to graph.

B: For bodies, cut two according to graph.

C: For arms #1 and #2, cut four each according to graphs.

D: For legs #1 and #2, cut four each according to graphs.

E: For elf collar, cut one according to graph.

F: For elf ears, cut two according to graph.

G: For hats #1 and #2, cut two each according to graphs.

H: For gift box #1 and #2 pieces, cut twelve (six for gift box #1 and six for gift box #2) 12 x 12 holes.

STITCHING INSTRUCTIONS:

1: Using colors and stitches indicated, work A, one B and C-H (two of each D and one of each G on opposite side of canvas) pieces according to graphs. Substituting dk. green for dk. red, work remaining B piece according to graph. With lt. pink, Overcast edges of F pieces.

2: Using black and Backstitch, embroider mouth on A pieces as indicated on graph.

3: For each head, with lt. pink, Whipstitch ends of one A together as indicated; Whipstitch X edges together as indicated. Glue hair and one small pom-pom for nose to head as indicated and as shown in photo.

NOTE: Cut one 2½"-across circle from each color of felt.

4: For each body, with matching color, Whipstitch ends of one B together as indicated; Whipstitch X edges together as indicated, filling with ½ cup gravel or other weight and fiberfill before closing. Glue matching color felt circle to bottom of body.

5: For each arm, holding two corresponding C pieces wrong sides together, with matching colors, Whipstitch together. For each leg, holding two corresponding D pieces wrong sides together, with matching colors, Whipstitch together.

6: For elf collar, with dk. red, Whipstitch ends of E together as indicated; Whipstitch X edges together as indicated. With dk. red, Overcast unfinished edges. Glue collar to elf body as shown.

7: For each hat, holding corresponding G pieces wrong sides together, with matching colors, Whipstitch together as indicated; Overcast unfinished edges. Stuff lightly with fiberfill and glue to corresponding head. Glue head assembly, arms and legs to corresponding bodies as shown. Glue ears to elf head as shown.

8: For each gift box, with dk. green for box #1 and white for box #2, Whipstitch corresponding H pieces together.

NOTE: Cut one 2-yd. length of gold ribbon.

9: Wrap 2-yd. ribbon around white gift box as

Roly-Poly Santa & Holly-Jolly Elf

CONTINUED FROM PAGE 27

shown; tie ends into a multi-looped bow as shown. Tie remaining gold ribbon into a multi-looped bow; glue to green box as shown. Glue each box to corresponding arms and body as shown. Tie green ribbon into a bow and trim ends; glue to elf collar as shown. Tack bells to elf hat, collar and boots as shown. Glue white pom-pom to Santa hat as shown.✧

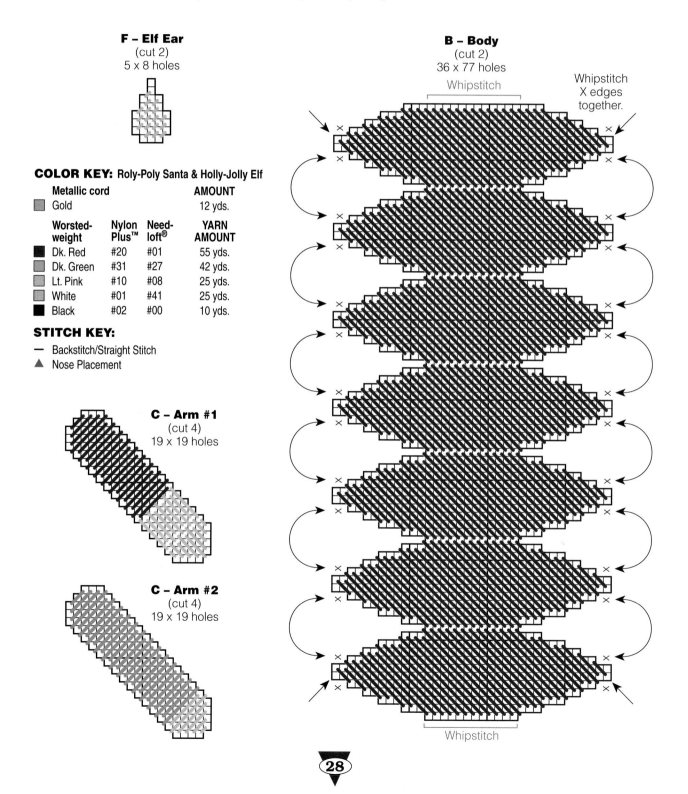

F – Elf Ear
(cut 2)
5 x 8 holes

B – Body
(cut 2)
36 x 77 holes

Whipstitch

Whipstitch X edges together.

COLOR KEY: Roly-Poly Santa & Holly-Jolly Elf

Metallic cord			AMOUNT
Gold			12 yds.

Worsted-weight	Nylon Plus™	Need-loft®	YARN AMOUNT
Dk. Red	#20	#01	55 yds.
Dk. Green	#31	#27	42 yds.
Lt. Pink	#10	#08	25 yds.
White	#01	#41	25 yds.
Black	#02	#00	10 yds.

STITCH KEY:

— Backstitch/Straight Stitch
▲ Nose Placement

C – Arm #1
(cut 4)
19 x 19 holes

C – Arm #2
(cut 4)
19 x 19 holes

Whipstitch

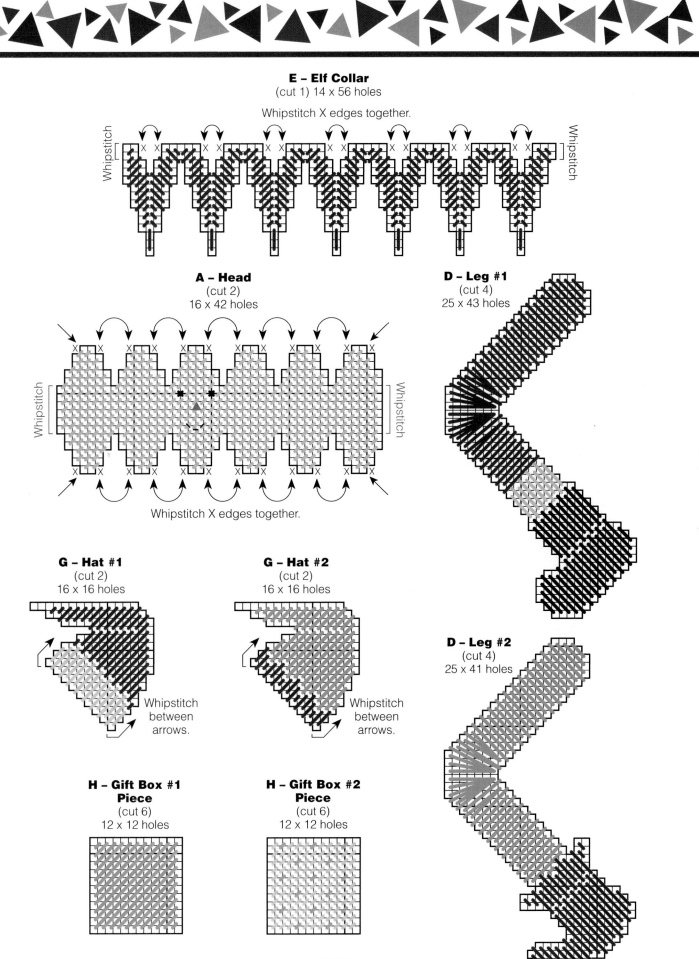

E – Elf Collar
(cut 1) 14 x 56 holes

Whipstitch X edges together.

Whipstitch

Whipstitch

A – Head
(cut 2)
16 x 42 holes

Whipstitch

Whipstitch

Whipstitch X edges together.

D – Leg #1
(cut 4)
25 x 43 holes

G – Hat #1
(cut 2)
16 x 16 holes

Whipstitch
between
arrows.

G – Hat #2
(cut 2)
16 x 16 holes

Whipstitch
between
arrows.

D – Leg #2
(cut 4)
25 x 41 holes

H – Gift Box #1 Piece
(cut 6)
12 x 12 holes

H – Gift Box #2 Piece
(cut 6)
12 x 12 holes

Happy Christmas

Designed by
Michele Wilcox

SIZE: 7¾" x 10⅝", not including ruffle.

MATERIALS: One sheet of 7-count plastic canvas; Four gold 8-mm jingle bells; 1¼ yds. red 1⅜" pleated ruffle; Craft glue or glue gun; Pearlized metallic cord (for amount see Color Key); #3 pearl cotton or six-strand embroidery floss (for amounts see Color Key); Worsted-weight or plastic canvas yarn (for amounts see Color Key).

CUTTING INSTRUCTIONS:

A: For Happy Christmas, cut one 50 x 70 holes.

STITCHING INSTRUCTIONS:

1: Using colors and stitches indicated, work A according to graph; fill in uncoded areas using dk. royal and Continental Stitch. With dk. royal, Overcast unfinished edges.

2: Using pearl cotton or six strands floss in colors indicated, Backstitch, French Knot and Fly Stitch, embroider facial detail, ear outlines and reins as indicated on graph.

NOTE: Cut one 9" length each of yellow and black pearl cotton or floss.

3: For rein ends, thread one end of yellow strand from front to back through one ▲ hole, then from back to front through remaining ▲ hole; pull ends to even. Tie a knot in each end close to canvas and trim, leaving 1½" tails on front. For sack tie, thread one end of black strand from front to back through one ✦ hole, then from back to front through remaining ✦

hole; pull ends to even. Tie ends into a bow as shown in photo.

4: Tack or glue bells to A as indicated. Glue ruffle to wrong side around edge as shown. Hang as desired.✧

COLOR KEY: Happy Christmas

Pearlized metallic cord			AMOUNT
▨ White			5 yds.

#3 pearl cotton or floss			AMOUNT
■ Black			2 yds.
■ Yellow			2 yds.

Worsted-weight	Nylon Plus™	Need-loft®	YARN AMOUNT
□ Dk. Royal	#07	#48	35 yds.
■ Dk. Red	#20	#01	9 yds.
▨ Camel	#34	#43	8 yds.
▨ Dk. Green	#31	#27	5 yds.
▨ Gray	#23	#38	2 yds.
▨ Tangerine	#15	#11	2 yds.
▨ Flesh	#14	#56	1 yd.

STITCH KEY:

— Backstitch/Straight Stitch
● French Knot
Y Fly Stitch
O Bell Attachment
▲ Reins Attachment
✦ Sack Tie Attachment

A – Happy Christmas (cut 1) 50 x 70 holes

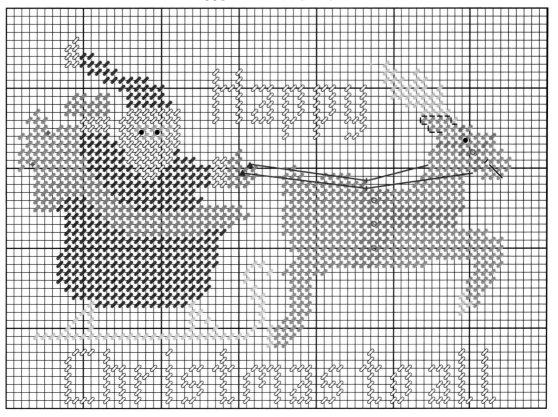

Fabric photographed with permission of Santee Print Works, Inc., New York, New York

Christmas Charm

Tinkling sleigh
bells and songs of
carolers fill the air. Evergreen
garlands drape the hearth and
snow falls gently, covering the yard …
So trim the tree, and create a Christmas
wonderland throughout your home using
handmade ornaments and accents.
From formal to lighthearted,
celebrate a different
holiday mood in every
nook and corner
of your
home.

Convey your season's greetings with gilded Victorian ribbon banners.

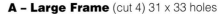

Sentiment Banners

Designed by Faye F. Gibbs

SIZE: Noel is 9" x 33"; Joy is 5⅛" x 28¾".

MATERIALS: Three sheets of white 7-count plastic canvas; 3¼ yds. burgundy 2¾" velveteen ribbon; Two 1½" gold metal rings; Seven gold articial holly sprigs; Sewing needle and burgundy thread; Craft glue or glue gun; Metallic cord (for amount see Color Key); Worsted-weight or plastic canvas yarn (for amount see Color Key).

CUTTING INSTRUCTIONS:

A: For large and small frames, cut four large and three small according to graphs.

B: For letters, cut one each according to graphs on page 36.

STITCHING INSTRUCTIONS:

NOTE: A pieces are unworked.

1: Using white and Continental Stitch, work B pieces. With cord, Whipstitch one letter centered to top and bottom cutout edges of each frame as indicated on graphs; Overcast unfinished edges of letters and frames.

NOTE: Cut ribbon into two 3", two 22", one 27" and one 32" length.

2: For each bow, with thread, sew one 3" and one 22" ribbon together according to Bow Assembly Diagram on page 36. For hangers, sew one ring and one bow to one end of 27" and 32" ribbons as shown in photo; trim ends as desired.

3: For Noel Banner, spacing frames as shown, glue frames to longer hanger to spell "Noel."

4: For Joy Banner, repeat Step 3 with remaining frames and hanger to spell "Joy."

5: Glue one holly sprig to each letter as shown.✧

COLOR KEY: Sentiment Banners

Metallic cord			AMOUNT
☐ White/Gold			35 yds.

Worsted-weight	Nylon Plus™	Need-loft®	YARN AMOUNT
☐ White	#01	#41	24 yds.

A – Small Frame (cut 3) 29 x 31 holes

Cut Out

A – Large Frame (cut 4) 31 x 33 holes

Cut Out

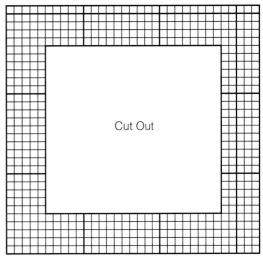

Sentiment Banners

PHOTO ON PAGE 34

B – Noel "N"
(cut 1) 17 x 21 holes

Whipstitch to large A.

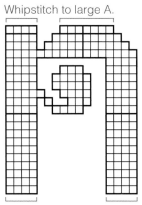

Whipstitch to large A.

B – Noel "O"
(cut 1) 17 x 21 holes

Whipstitch to large A.

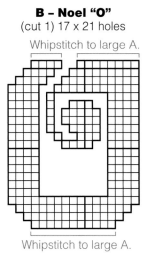

Whipstitch to large A.

Bow Assembly Diagram

Step 1:
Overlapping ends 2", loop ends of one 22" ribbon to center.

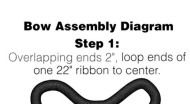

22"
Ribbon

2" Overlap

Whipstitch to large A.

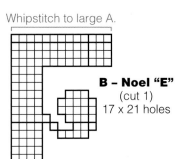

B – Noel "E"
(cut 1)
17 x 21 holes

Whipstitch to large A.

Whipstitch to large A.

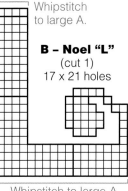

B – Noel "L"
(cut 1)
17 x 21 holes

Whipstitch to large A.

Step 2:
Fold 3" ribbon in half lengthwise; wrap around center of 22" ribbon and sew at back to secure.

3" Ribbon

B – Joy "J"
(cut 1)
19 x 21 holes

Whipstitch to small A.

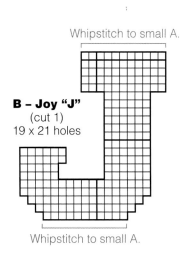

Whipstitch to small A.

B – Joy "O"
(cut 1) 19 x 21 holes

Whipstitch to small A.

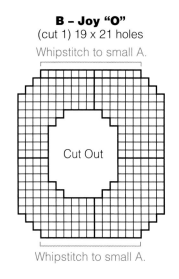

Cut Out

Whipstitch to small A.

B – Joy "Y"
(cut 1) 19 x 21 holes

Whipstitch to small A.

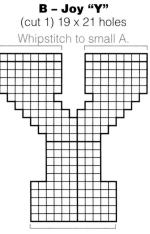

Whipstitch to small A.

Dazzling Trio

Designed by Mary T. Cosgrove

Instructions on next page

Dazzling Trio

PHOTO ON PAGE 37

SIZE: Each is about 3" x 4".

MATERIALS: One sheet of red and scraps of clear 7-count plastic canvas; One 4¼" plastic canvas circle; Two 4¼" circles of red felt; One gold 10-mm jingle bell; One gold 1" metal ring; 132 red seed beads; Monofilament fishing line; Craft glue or glue gun; 1 yd. red six-strand embroidery floss; 2 yds. green ⅛" metallic ribbon; Metallic cord (for amounts see Color Key); Worsted-weight or plastic canvas yarn (for amounts see Color Key).

DATED BELL

CUTTING INSTRUCTIONS:

A: For Bell dome, cut one from red 2 x 60 holes (no graph).

B: For Bell bottom, cut one from red 2 x 25 holes (no graph).

C: For Bell date, cut one from red according to graph of choice.

STITCHING INSTRUCTIONS:

1: Using gold cord and Continental Stitch, work A and B pieces; using white and stitches indicated, work C according to graph. Do not Overcast unfinished edges.

2: For Bell, Whipstitch ends of A and B pieces together. Using a blow-dry hair dryer set on low heat, soften canvas to form bell shape. With fishing line, sew C to inside of Bell and jingle bell to bottom as shown in photo.

NOTE: Cut three 12" lengths of metallic ribbon.

3: Holding 12" ribbons together, tie into a bow; sew bow to top of Bell.

EVERGREEN GLOBE

CUTTING INSTRUCTIONS:

A: For Globe, cut one from red according to graph.

B: For Globe tree, cut two from clear according to graph.

STITCHING INSTRUCTIONS:

1: Using gold cord and Continental Stitch, work A according to graph; overlapping ends, work through both thicknesses as one piece to join. Using green and Continental Stitch, work B pieces according to graph.

NOTE: Separate floss into single-ply strands.

2: For each garland string on each B piece, with one strand floss, thread needle from back to front at one ◆ hole as indicated on graph, thread on half the number of beads indicated below, tack string to center point as indicated, thread on remaining number of beads, thread needle from front to back at ◆ hole on opposite side; knot ends on wrong side. For top row garland, string 14 beads; for center garland, string 22 beads; and for bottom garland, string 30 beads.

3: Holding B pieces wrong sides together, with green, Whipstitch together. With fishing line, attach top of tree to inside top of Globe. For hanger, attach a loop of gold cord to top as shown in photo.

DOVE OF PEACE

CUTTING INSTRUCTIONS:

A: For cage bars, cut one from red accordng to Globe A graph.

B: For cage bottom, use 4¼" circle (no graph).

C: For dove body, cut two from clear according to graph.

D: For dove wings, cut four from clear according to graph.

E: For dove tail, cut two from clear according to graph.

STITCHING INSTRUCTIONS:

1: Using gold cord and Continental Stitch, work A according to graph. Whipstitch ends of A to edge of B at equal distances around circle; Overcast unfinished edges of B. Glue one felt circle to top and one to bottom of B.

2: Using white and stitches indicated, work C-E (one C, one E and two D pieces on opposite side of canvas) pieces according to graphs. Using black cord and French Knot, embroider eyes as indicated on C graph.

3: For each wing, body and tail, holding match-

ing pieces wrong sides together, with gold for beak on body as shown in photo and with white, Whipstitch C-E pieces together. Tack wings and tail to body as shown.

4: With fishing line, attach dove at top center of body to inside top of cage; sew ring to top of cage.

NOTE: Cut three 12" lengths of metallic ribbon.

5: Holding 12" ribbons together, tie into a bow around ring; trim ends.✧

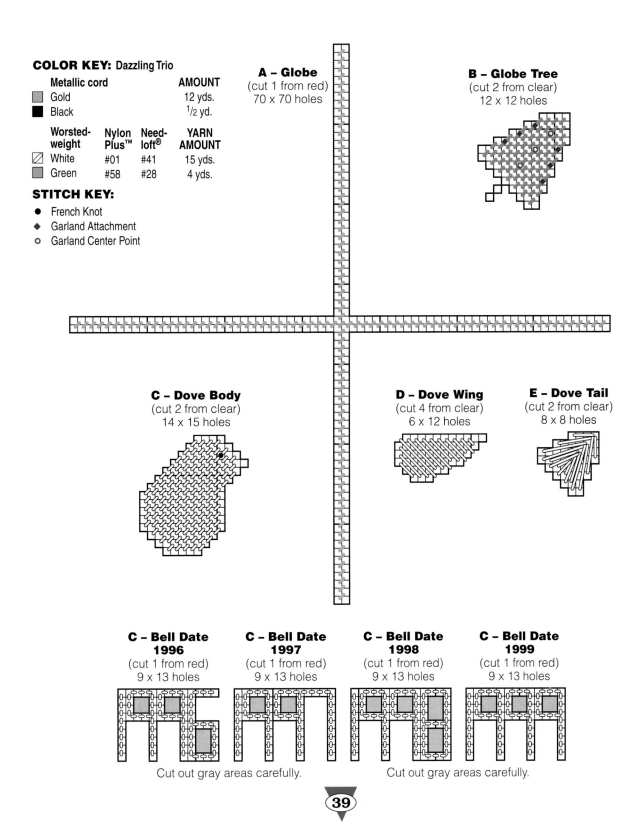

COLOR KEY: Dazzling Trio

Metallic cord			AMOUNT
▨ Gold			12 yds.
■ Black			½ yd.

Worsted-weight	Nylon Plus™	Need-loft®	YARN AMOUNT
▨ White	#01	#41	15 yds.
▨ Green	#58	#28	4 yds.

STITCH KEY:

- ● French Knot
- ◆ Garland Attachment
- ○ Garland Center Point

A – Globe
(cut 1 from red)
70 x 70 holes

B – Globe Tree
(cut 2 from clear)
12 x 12 holes

C – Dove Body
(cut 2 from clear)
14 x 15 holes

D – Dove Wing
(cut 4 from clear)
6 x 12 holes

E – Dove Tail
(cut 2 from clear)
8 x 8 holes

C – Bell Date 1996
(cut 1 from red)
9 x 13 holes

C – Bell Date 1997
(cut 1 from red)
9 x 13 holes

C – Bell Date 1998
(cut 1 from red)
9 x 13 holes

C – Bell Date 1999
(cut 1 from red)
9 x 13 holes

Cut out gray areas carefully.

Cut out gray areas carefully.

39

Old World Santas

Designed by Eve Andrade

Add an old-fashioned touch with five festive Santas ready to hang as ornaments or hold candy sticks.

SIZE: Each is about 1¾" x 5".

MATERIALS FOR ONE: ½ sheet of 14-count plastic canvas; Two coordinating color seed beads; One pink or red 3 - 4-mm pom-pom; ⅛ - ¼" satin ribbon (optional); Craft novelties, pom-poms, decorative charms or miniatures (optional); Craft glue or glue gun; #5 pearl cotton or six-strand embroidery floss (for amounts see individual Color Keys on pages 41-44); Medium metallic braid or metallic ribbon (for amounts see individual Color Keys).

NOTE: For optional pom-pom teddy bear miniature, glue two 12-mm and six 8-mm tan

COLOR KEY: Crimson Santa

#5 pearl cotton or floss		AMOUNT
■ White		10 yds.
▨ Flesh		½ yd.

Medium metallic braid or ribbon	Kreinik (#16)	YARN AMOUNT
■ Red	#003HL	11 yds.
▨ Garnet	#080HL	5 yds.
■ Black	#005HL	3 yds.
▨ Gold	#002	½ yd.
▨ Seafoam	#2829	½ yd.

STITCH KEY:

- — Backstitch/Straight Stitch
- ✦ Rya Knot
- ○ Eye Attachment

A – Crimson Santa Front
(cut 1)
22 x 69 holes

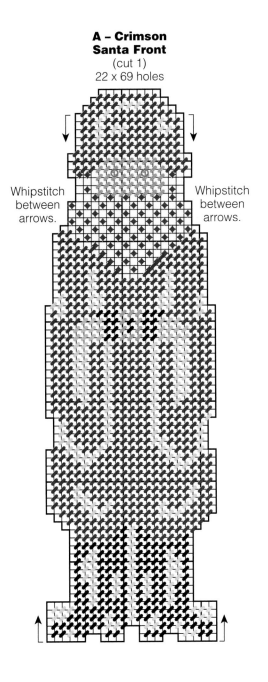

Whipstitch between arrows.

Whipstitch between arrows.

A – Crimson Santa Back
(cut 1)
22 x 69 holes

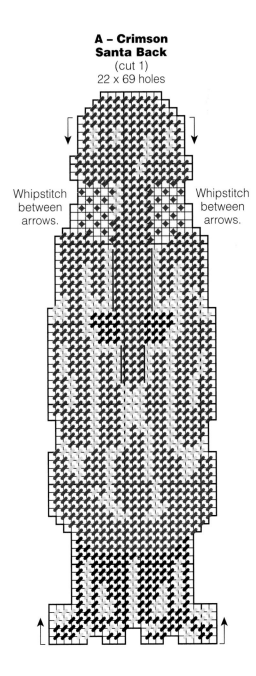

Whipstitch between arrows.

Whipstitch between arrows.

Old World Santas

CONTINUED FROM PAGE 41

pom-poms together according to Teddy Bear Assembly Diagram. For eyes, glue on seed beads. If desired, tie a length of braid or ribbon into a bow around neck; trim ends.

CUTTING INSTRUCTIONS:

NOTE: Graphs continued on page 44.

A: For Crimson Santa front and back, cut one each according to graphs on page 41.

B: For Emerald Santa front and back, cut one each according to graphs.

C: For Amethyst Santa front and back, cut one each according to graphs.

D: For Sapphire Santa front and back, cut one each according to graphs.

E: For Victorian Santa front and back, cut one each according to graphs.

STITCHING INSTRUCTIONS:

1: Using pearl cotton or six strands floss and braid or ribbon in colors and stitches indicated,

**B – Emerald
Santa Front**
(cut 1)
20 x 72 holes

**B – Emerald
Santa Back**
(cut 1)
20 x 72 holes

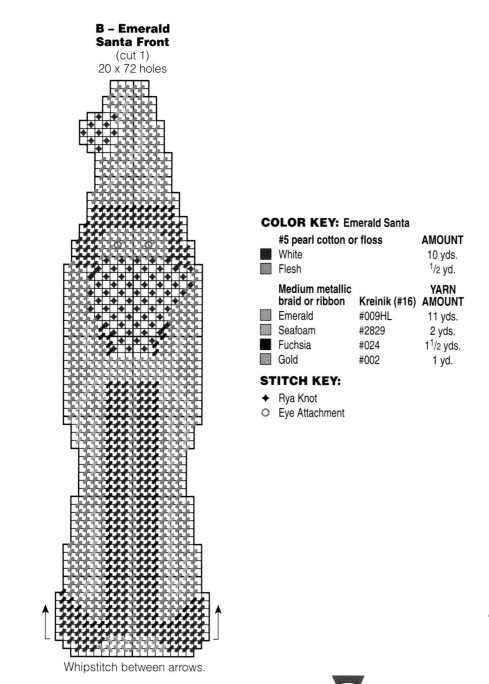

COLOR KEY: Emerald Santa

#5 pearl cotton or floss		AMOUNT
White		10 yds.
Flesh		1/2 yd.

Medium metallic braid or ribbon	Kreinik (#16)	YARN AMOUNT
Emerald	#009HL	11 yds.
Seafoam	#2829	2 yds.
Fuchsia	#024	1 1/2 yds.
Gold	#002	1 yd.

STITCH KEY:

✦ Rya Knot
○ Eye Attachment

Whipstitch between arrows.

Whipstitch between arrows.

work front and back pieces according to graphs of choice. Using white and Rya Knot for hair and beard (leave ¼ - ¾" loops) and colors indicated, Backstitch and Straight Stitch for cloak detail on Crimson and Victorian Santas, embroider as indicated on graphs. Omitting Emerald Santa, clip through Rya Knot loops; trim strands to even. Fray strands to fluff, if desired.

2: Using a single strand of flesh, sew beads for eyes to front as indicated. If desired, tack novelties and/or charms to front and back. Holding front and back pieces wrong sides together, with matching colors as shown in photo, Whipstitch together as indicated; Overcast unfinished edges. Glue pink or red pom-pom to face for nose as shown. Hang as desired, or use to hold candy sticks.✧

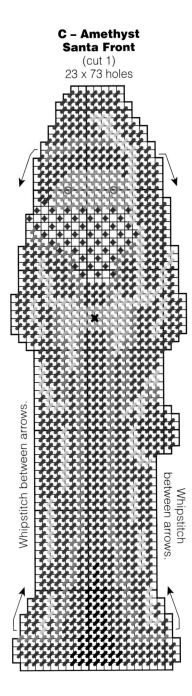

C – Amethyst Santa Front
(cut 1)
23 x 73 holes

C – Amethyst Santa Back
(cut 1)
23 x 73 holes

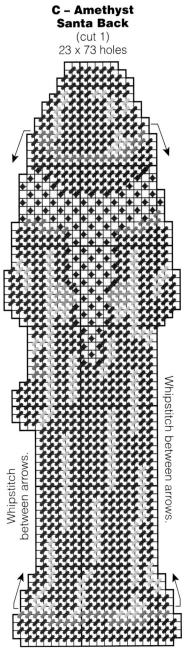

COLOR KEY: Amethyst Santa

#5 pearl cotton or floss		AMOUNT
White		9 yds.
Flesh		½ yd.

Medium metallic braid or ribbon	Kreinik (#16)	YARN AMOUNT
Purple	#012HL	12 yds.
Confetti Fuchsia	#042	3 yds.
Sapphire	#051HL	3 yds.
Black	#005HL	2 yds.
Gold	#002	1 yd.
Seafoam	#2829	¼ yd.

STITCH KEY:
✦ Rya Knot
○ Eye Attachment

Whipstitch between arrows.

Teddy Bear Assembly Diagram

8-mm Pom-Pom

12-mm Pom-Pom

Old World Santas

PHOTO ON PAGE 40

COLOR KEY: Sapphire Santa

#5 pearl cotton or floss			AMOUNT
■	White		8 yds.
▨	Flesh		¹/₂ yd.

Medium metallic braid or ribbon		Kreinik (#16)	YARN AMOUNT
▨	Blue	#006HL	11 yds.
▨	Sapphire	#051HL	3 yds.
▨	Gold	#002	2 yds.
■	Black	#005HL	1 yds.
▨	Garnet	#080HL	¹/₂ yd.
▨	Seafoam	#2829	¹/₂ yd.

STITCH KEY:
- ✦ Rya Knot
- ○ Eye Attachment

COLOR KEY: Victorian Santa

#5 pearl cotton or floss			AMOUNT
■	White		8 yds.
▨	Flesh		¹/₂ yd.

Medium metallic braid or ribbon		Kreinik (#16)	YARN AMOUNT
■	Fuchsia	#024	11 yds.
▨	Confetti Fuchsia	#042	3 yds.
▨	Emerald	#009HL	2 yds.
▨	Purple	#012HL	1 yds.
■	Black	#005HL	¹/₂ yd.
▨	Seafoam	#2829	¹/₂ yd.
▨	Gold	#002	¹/₄ yd.

STITCH KEY:
- — Backstitch/Straight Stitch
- ✦ Rya Knot
- ○ Eye Attachment

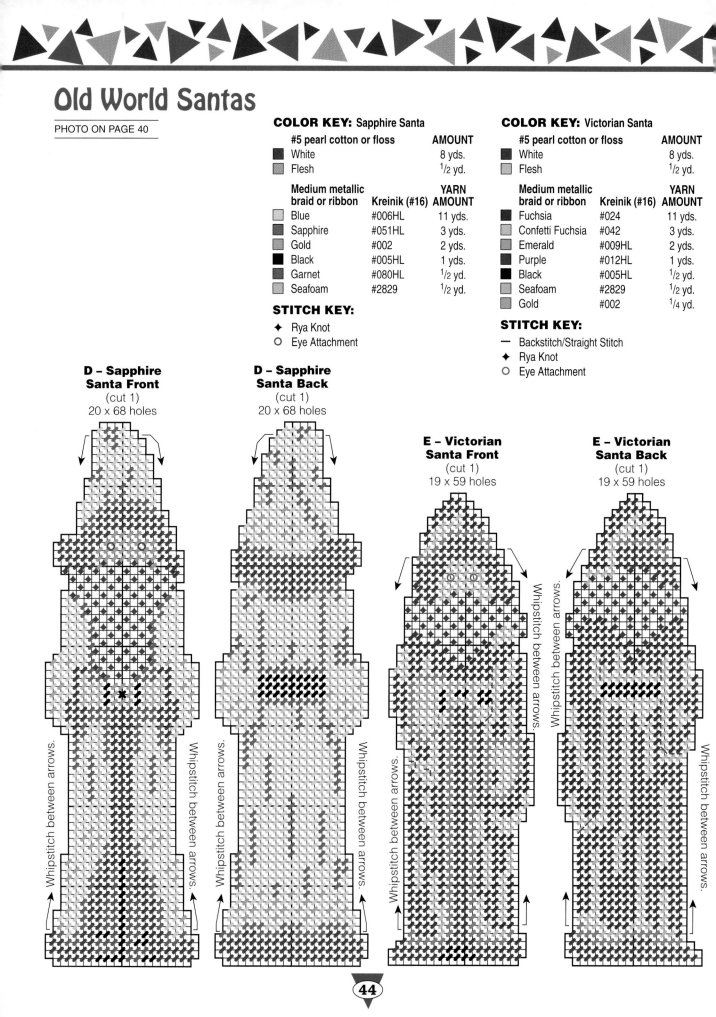

D – Sapphire Santa Front
(cut 1)
20 x 68 holes

D – Sapphire Santa Back
(cut 1)
20 x 68 holes

E – Victorian Santa Front
(cut 1)
19 x 59 holes

E – Victorian Santa Back
(cut 1)
19 x 59 holes

Whipstitch between arrows.

North Pole Cottage

Designed by Gina Woods

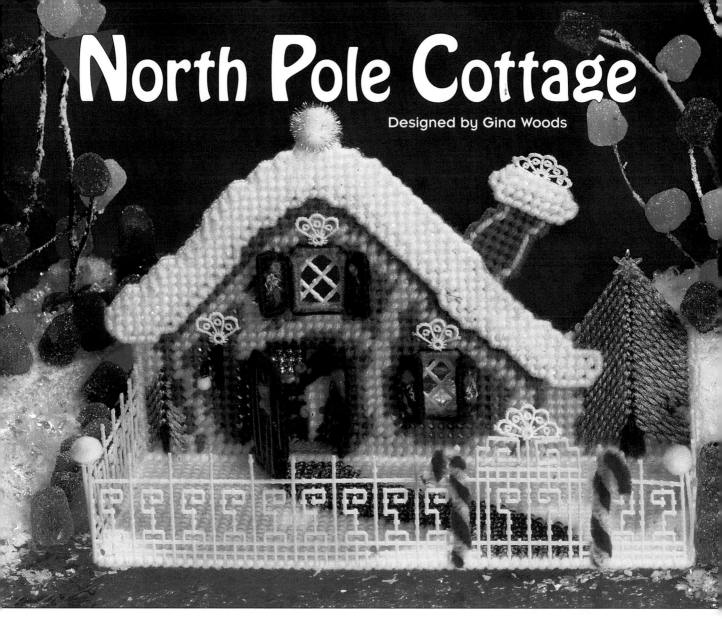

SIZE: 4½" x 8⅞" x 5¾" tall.

MATERIALS: One sheet of stiff, ½ sheet of white and scraps of black and pink 7-count plastic canvas; One white ¾" tinsel pom-pom; One 5-mm and two 10-mm white pom-poms; One white and one red 12" chenille stem; One lt. green 12-mm starflake bead; Five white ½-1" scalloped lace motifs; Clear glitter; Craft glue or glue gun; Metallic cord (for amounts see Color Key on page 46); Six-strand embroidery floss (for amounts see Color Key); Worsted-weight or plastic canvas yarn (for amounts see Color Key).

CUTTING INSTRUCTIONS:

NOTE: Graphs on pages 46 & 47.

A: For back, cut one from stiff according to graph.

B: For bottom, cut one from stiff 24 x 58 holes.

C: For shutters, cut four from stiff according to graph.

D: For roof trim, cut one from stiff according to graph.

E: For door, cut one from stiff according to graph.

F: For chimney, cut one from stiff according to graph.

G: For chimney trim, cut one from stiff according to graph.

H: For entry back wall, cut one from stiff 13 x 14 holes.

I: For entry side walls, cut two from stiff 4 x 14 holes (no graph).

J: For entry ceiling and floor, cut two (one for ceiling and one for floor) from stiff 4 x 13 holes (no graphs).

K: For window panes, cut two from pink

North Pole Cottage

CONTINUED FROM PAGE 45

according to graph.

   L: For lamp, cut one from black according to graph.

   M: For fence front, cut one from white according to graph.

   N: For fence sides, cut two from white according to graph.

STITCHING INSTRUCTIONS:

NOTE: K-N pieces are unworked.

1: Using colors and stitches indicated, work A, B, C (two on opposite side of canvas), E, F and H pieces according to graphs; fill in uncoded areas of A and B and work D and G pieces using white and Continental Stitch. With white, Overcast edges of D and G pieces. Fill in uncoded areas of H and work I and one J for ceiling using lemon and Continental Stitch. Using pink and Continental Stitch, work remaining J for floor.

2: Using yarn, cord and six strands floss in colors indicated, Straight Stitch, Backstitch and French Knot, embroider detail on A, C, E, F and H pieces as indicated on graphs. With pink, Overcast window cutout edges of A. With cinnamon, Whipstitch C and E pieces to A as indi-

cated; Overcast unfinished edges of shutters, doors and door cutout.

3: With camel for floor edges and with lemon, Whipstitch H-J pieces together according to Entry Assembly Diagram; Overcast unfinished edges.

4: With black, Whipstitch L to A as indicated. With sail blue at door end of A and with white, Whipstitch A, B, M and N pieces together (Do not join front and side fence edges together.); with white for large tree side and with matching colors (Omit tree top edges.), Overcast unfinished edges of A.

5: Glue D to right side and F to wrong side of A, entry to wrong side of A at door cutout and one K to wrong side of A at each window cutout. Glue G to F as shown in photo. Glue small pom-pom to bottom edge of lamp for bulb and tinsel pom-pom to roof as shown. Glue one 10-mm pom-pom to each corner of fence, lace motifs to house and chimney and bead to large tree top as shown.

6: For candy canes, twist chenille stems together; cut in half. Bend each section into cane shape; glue one candy cane to each side of gate as shown. ✧

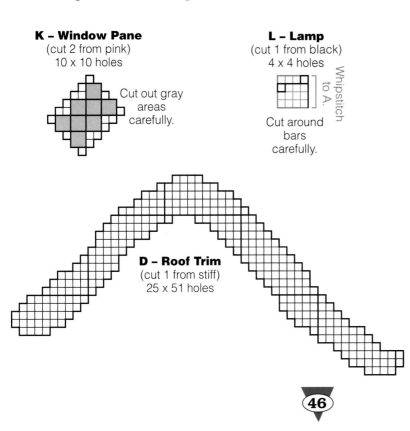

K – Window Pane
(cut 2 from pink)
10 x 10 holes

Cut out gray areas carefully.

L – Lamp
(cut 1 from black)
4 x 4 holes

Whipstitch to A.

Cut around bars carefully.

D – Roof Trim
(cut 1 from stiff)
25 x 51 holes

COLOR KEY: North Pole Cottage

Metallic cord			AMOUNT
Silver			1 yd.
Gold			½ yd.

Embroidery floss			AMOUNT
Black			2 yds.
Camel			2 yds.
Med. Brown			2 yds.
Pink			1 yd.
Red			1 yd.

Worsted-weight	Nylon Plus™	Need-loft®	YARN AMOUNT
White	#01	#41	40 yds.
Fern	#57	#23	15 yds.
Camel	#34	#43	12 yds.
Cinnamon	#44	#14	9 yds.
Lt. Pink	#10	#08	9 yds.
Lemon	#25	#20	8 yds.
Lt. Blue	#05	#36	5 yds.
Pink	#11	#07	4 yds.
Gold	#27	#17	2 yds.
Black	#02	#00	1 yd.

STITCH KEY:

— Backstitch/Straight Stitch
● French Knot
☐ Unworked Area/Shutter Attachment
☐ Door Attachment
✦ Lamp Attachment

C – Shutter
(cut 4 from stiff)
3 x 6 holes

Whipstitch to A.

E – Door
(cut 1 from stiff)
10 x 12 holes

Whipstitch to A.

Cut out gray area.

F – Chimney
(cut 1 from stiff)
9 x 16 holes

A – Back
(cut 1 from stiff)
33 x 61 holes

Cut Out

Cut Out

Cut Out

B – Bottom
(cut 1 from stiff) 24 x 58 holes

G – Chimney Trim
(cut 1 from stiff)
3 x 9 holes

H – Entry Back Wall
(cut 1 from stiff)
13 x 14 holes

N – Fence Side
(cut 2 from white) 10 x 24 holes

Cut out gray areas and
around bars carefully.

Entry Assembly Diagram

Ceiling J

I

H

I

Floor J

M – Fence Front (cut 1 from white) 14 x 58 holes

Cut out gray areas and around bars carefully.

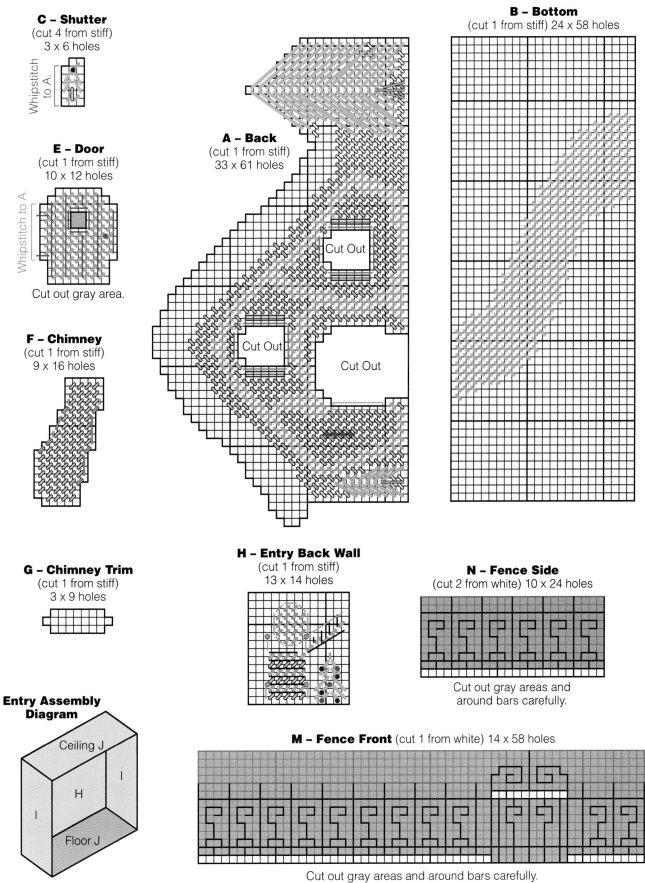

Angels Around the World

Designed by Terry A. Ricioli

SIZE: Each Coaster is 4⅝" x 4¾"; Coaster Holder is 1⅜" x 5⅜" x 1⅞" tall; Ornament is 4⅝" x 4¾"; Centerpiece is about 6" across x 4⅝" tall.

MATERIALS: Two sheets of 7-count plastic canvas; ½ yd. medium metallic braid; Six-strand embroidery floss (for amounts see Color Key on page 50); Metallic cord (for amount see Color Key); Worsted-weight or plastic canvas yarn (for amounts see Color Key).

NOTE: Graphs continued on page 50.

COASTERS & HOLDER

CUTTING INSTRUCTIONS:

A: For Coasters #1-#4, cut one each according to graphs.

B: For Holder sides, cut two according to graph.

C: For Holder ends, cut two 5 x 8 holes (no graph).

D: For Holder bottom, cut one 8 x 28 holes (no graph).

STITCHING INSTRUCTIONS:

NOTE: D piece is unworked.

1: Using colors and stitches indicated, work A and B pieces according to graphs; with face color for faces and with matching colors as shown in photo, Overcast unfinished edges of A pieces. Using white and Slanted Gobelin Stitch over narrow width, work C pieces.

2: For Holder, with white, Whipstitch B-D pieces together as indicated on B graph; Overcast unfinished edges.

3: Using six strands floss in colors indicated and Straight Stitch, embroider facial detail on A pieces as indicated.

4: For pony tails, with matching hair color, leaving 1" tails, work one Lark's Head Knot on each side of each A as indicated.

NOTE: Cut two 9" lengths each of pink, lt. green, lt. blue and lavender floss.

5: Tie one coordinating color of cut floss into a bow around each pony tail as shown; trim floss ends. Brush yarn ends to fluff as shown.

ORNAMENT

CUTTING INSTRUCTIONS:

A: For Ornament front, cut one according to Coasters & Holder A #1 graph.

B: For Ornament back, cut one according to graph.

STITCHING INSTRUCTIONS:

1: Using colors and stitches indicated, work A and B pieces according to graphs.

2: Using six strands floss in colors indicated and Straight Stitch, embroider facial detail on A as indicated on graph.

3: Holding A and B pieces wrong sides together, with cinnamon for head and with matching colors as shown in photo, Whipstitch together.

4: For pony tails, using lt. blue floss to tie hair and working Lark's Head Knots through both thicknesses as indicated, follow Steps 4 and 5 of Coasters & Holder.

5: For hanger, thread metallic braid through center top hole; tie ends together.

CENTERPIECE

CUTTING INSTRUCTIONS:

A: For angels #1-#4, cut one each according to Coasters & Holder A graphs.

STITCHING INSTRUCTIONS:

1: Overlapping bottom corners of each piece as indicated in Dress Overlap Illustration and working through both thicknesses at overlap areas as one piece to join angels into ring, using colors and stitches indicated, work A pieces according to graphs. With face color for faces and with matching colors as shown, Overcast unfinished edges.

2: Follow Steps 3-5 of Coasters & Holder. ✧

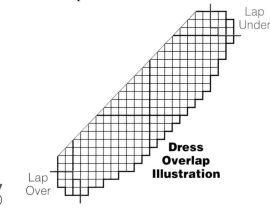

Lap Under

Lap Over

Dress Overlap Illustration

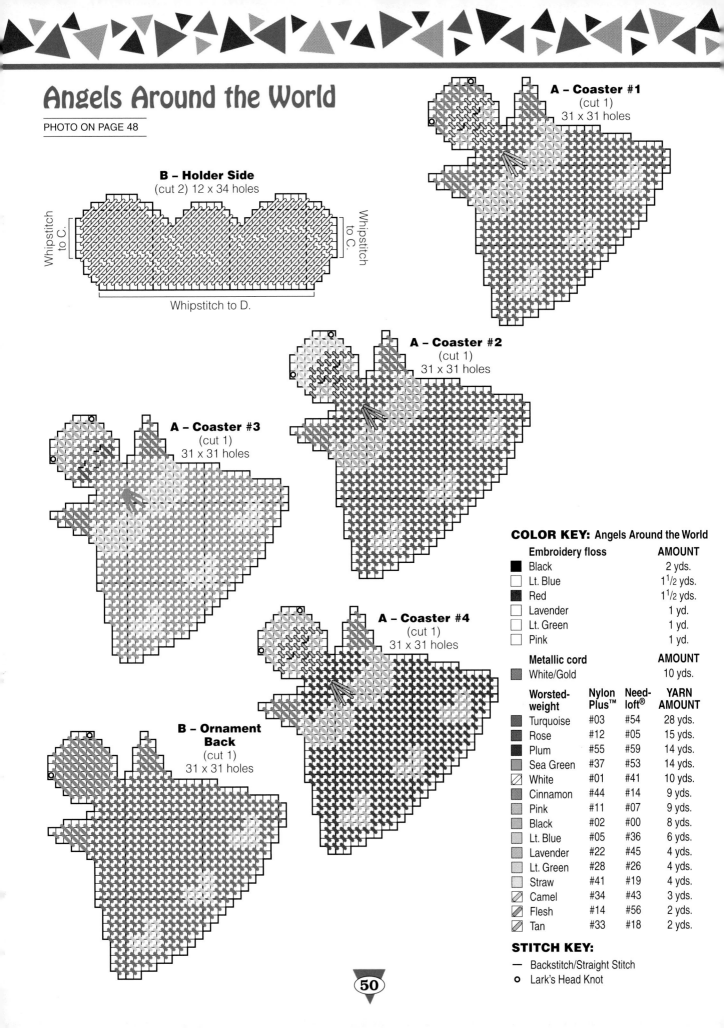

Angels Around the World

PHOTO ON PAGE 48

B – Holder Side
(cut 2) 12 x 34 holes

Whipstitch to C.

Whipstitch to C.

Whipstitch to D.

A – Coaster #1
(cut 1)
31 x 31 holes

A – Coaster #2
(cut 1)
31 x 31 holes

A – Coaster #3
(cut 1)
31 x 31 holes

A – Coaster #4
(cut 1)
31 x 31 holes

B – Ornament Back
(cut 1)
31 x 31 holes

COLOR KEY: Angels Around the World

Embroidery floss			AMOUNT
Black			2 yds.
Lt. Blue			1 1/2 yds.
Red			1 1/2 yds.
Lavender			1 yd.
Lt. Green			1 yd.
Pink			1 yd.

Metallic cord			AMOUNT
White/Gold			10 yds.

Worsted-weight	Nylon Plus™	Need-loft®	YARN AMOUNT
Turquoise	#03	#54	28 yds.
Rose	#12	#05	15 yds.
Plum	#55	#59	14 yds.
Sea Green	#37	#53	14 yds.
White	#01	#41	10 yds.
Cinnamon	#44	#14	9 yds.
Pink	#11	#07	9 yds.
Black	#02	#00	8 yds.
Lt. Blue	#05	#36	6 yds.
Lavender	#22	#45	4 yds.
Lt. Green	#28	#26	4 yds.
Straw	#41	#19	4 yds.
Camel	#34	#43	3 yds.
Flesh	#14	#56	2 yds.
Tan	#33	#18	2 yds.

STITCH KEY:
— Backstitch/Straight Stitch
o Lark's Head Knot

North Star Nativity

Designed by Cherie Marie Leck

SIZE: 3¾" x 10⅛" x 9⅜" tall.

MATERIALS: Three sheets of 7-count plastic canvas; One light cord assembly with snap-in socket and switch (available at most ceramic shops); One white 7-watt Christmas bulb; Worsted-weight or plastic canvas yarn (for amounts see Color Key on page 52).

CUTTING INSTRUCTIONS:

A: For front and back, cut one each according to graph on page 52.

B: For side pieces, cut two 23 x 82 holes (no graph).

North Star Nativity

CONTINUED FROM PAGE 51

STITCHING INSTRUCTIONS:

1: Using dk. royal and Continental Stitch, work solid A for front according to graph; fill in uncoded areas and work back A using lt. silver and Continental Stitch. Using dk. royal and Backstitch, embroider star on front as indicated on graph.

2: Using dk. royal and Slanted Gobelin Stitch over nine bars, work B pieces according to Side Stitch Pattern Guide; Whipstitch A and B pieces together according to Nativity Assembly Diagram.

3: Insert bulb through back cutout; secure to canvas according to manufacturer's instructions.✧

Side Stitch Pattern Guide

Continue established pattern across each entire piece.

STITCH KEY:
— Backstitch/Straight Stitch
☐ Cutout for back only.

COLOR KEY: North Star Nativity

	Worsted-weight	Nylon Plus™	Need-loft®	YARN AMOUNT
☐	Lt. Silver		#65	80 yds.
▨	Dk. Royal	#07	#48	68 yds.

Nativity Assembly Diagram
(back view)

A – Front & Back
(cut 1 each) 61 x 66 holes

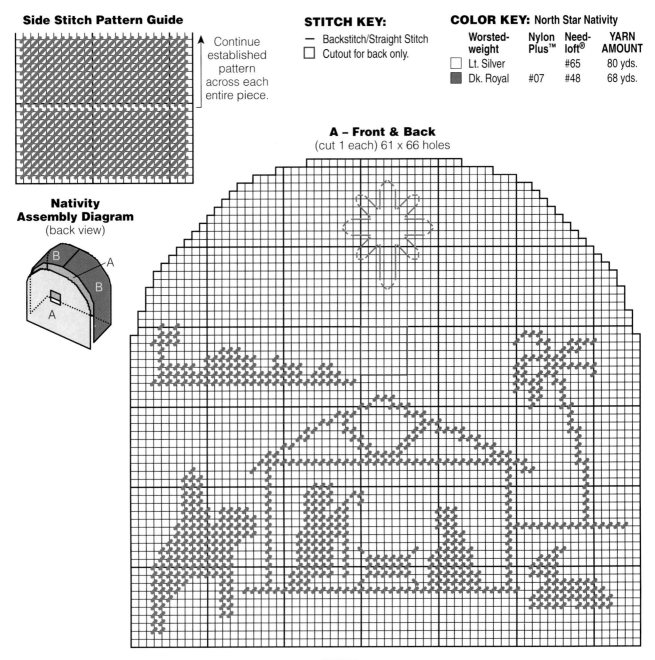

Glittery Centerpiece

Designed by Jody Flynn

SIZE: 5" x 5" x 9¼" tall.

MATERIALS: Six Uniek® Crafts 5" plastic canvas hexagon shapes; One 3" plastic canvas radial circle; ½ sheet of 7-count plastic canvas; Four gold 10-mm round faceted acrylic stones; Craft glue or glue gun; Metallic cord (for amounts see Color Key).

CUTTING INSTRUCTIONS:

NOTE: Graphs continued on page 57.

A: For sides, use four hexagon shapes. (**NOTE:** Cut hanger loops off.)

B: For top and bottom corners, cut eight triangles from remaining hexagon shapes (no graph).

C: For top and bottom, cut two (one for top and one for bottom) 18 x 18 holes.

D: For ring base side, cut one 8 x 53 holes (no graph).

E: For ring base top, cut away outer two rows of holes from 3" circle according to graph.

F: For ring, cut two 2 x 45 holes (no graph).

STITCHING INSTRUCTIONS:

1: Using colors and stitches indicated, work four A pieces according to graph; using red/silver and white/gold, work four B pieces in each color according to pattern established on A graph.

2: Using white/silver and stitches indicated, work C and E pieces according to graphs. Overlapping six holes at ends and working through both thicknesses at overlap area to join, using white/silver and Long Stitch over narrow width, work D.

CONTINUED ON PAGE 57

C – Top & Bottom
(cut 1 each) 18 x 18 holes

COLOR KEY: Glittery Centerpiece

Metallic cord	AMOUNT
White/Silver	35 yds.
Red/Silver	9 yds.
White/Gold	9 yds.
Blue/Silver	5 yds.
Green/Silver	5 yds.
Orange/Silver	5 yds.
Purple/Silver	5 yds.

E – Ring Base Top
(cut 1 from 3" circle)

Cut away gray area.

Continue established pattern across entire piece.

Ring Stitch Pattern Guide

Continue established pattern around entire piece.

Santa's Cabin

**Designed by
Nancy W. Dorman**

SIZE: 4⅞" x 5⅝" x 5¼" tall.

MATERIALS: 1½ sheets of 7-count plastic canvas; One green 12" tinsel stem; Craft glue or glue gun; Six-strand embroidery floss (for amounts see Color Key); Worsted-weight or plastic canvas yarn (for amounts see Color Key).

CUTTING INSTRUCTIONS:

A: For house front and back, cut one each according to graphs.

B: For house sides, cut two 18 x 26 holes.

C: For shutters, cut ten 2 x 6 holes.

D: For door trim, cut one according to graph.

E: For roof sides, cut two according to graph.

F: For roof front and back trim, cut two (one for front and one for back) according to graph.

G: For roof side trim, cut two according to graph.

H: For chimney front and back, cut two (one for front and one for back) according to graph.

I: For chimney sides, cut two 5 x 6 holes.

J: For base, cut one according to graph.

STITCHING INSTRUCTIONS:

NOTE: Use a doubled strand for Overcast; use Herringbone Whipstitch for Whipstitch.

1: Using colors and stitches indicated, work A-J pieces according to graphs; with matching colors, Overcast edges of C, D and J pieces. Using yarn and six strands floss in colors indicated, Backstitch and French Knot, embroider detail as indicated on A and B graphs.

2: With dk. green, Overcast cutout edges of A pieces; Whipstitch A and B pieces together. With white for bottom edges and with dk. green, Overcast unfinished edges of house.

3: With matching colors, Whipstitch and assemble E-I pieces as indicated and according to Roof & Chimney Assembly Diagram; with white, Overcast unfinished edges.

4: With white, tack house to center of base; set roof on house.

NOTES: Cut six 1¾" lengths of tinsel stem; bend each length into a circle. Cut red floss into six 9" lengths; tie each 9" strand into a small bow and trim ends.

5: Glue one tinsel wreath to each window and to door; glue one bow to top of each wreath as shown.✧

A – Front
(cut 1)
19 x 27 holes

Cut out gray area carefully.

A – Back
(cut 1)
19 x 27 holes

Cut out gray area carefully.

B – Side (cut 2) 18 x 26 holes

COLOR KEY: Santa's Cabin

Embroidery floss			AMOUNT
■ Dk. Brown			2 yds.
□ Red			1 1/2 yds.

Worsted-weight	Nylon Plus™	Need-loft®	YARN AMOUNT
■ White	#01	#41	50 yds.
■ Dk. Green	#31	#27	38 yds.
■ Red	#19	#02	12 yds.
■ Lt. Silver		#65	5 yds.

STITCH KEY:
— Backstitch/Straight Stitch
● French Knot

C – Shutter
(cut 10)
2 x 6 holes

D – Door Trim
(cut 1)
5 x 9 holes

F – Roof Front & Back Trim
(cut 1 each)
18 x 18 holes

H – Chimney Front & Back
(cut 1 each)
5 x 6 holes

I – Chimney Side
(cut 2)
5 x 6 holes

G – Roof Side Trim (cut 2) 2 x 29 holes

E – Roof Side (cut 2) 17 x 29 holes
Whipstitch   Whipstitch

J – Base
(cut 1)
44 x 44 holes

Roof & Chimney Assembly Diagram

Step 1:
Whipstitch H and I pieces together.

Step 2:
Whipstitch E-G pieces together.

Step 3:
Tack bottom of chimney to center top of roof.

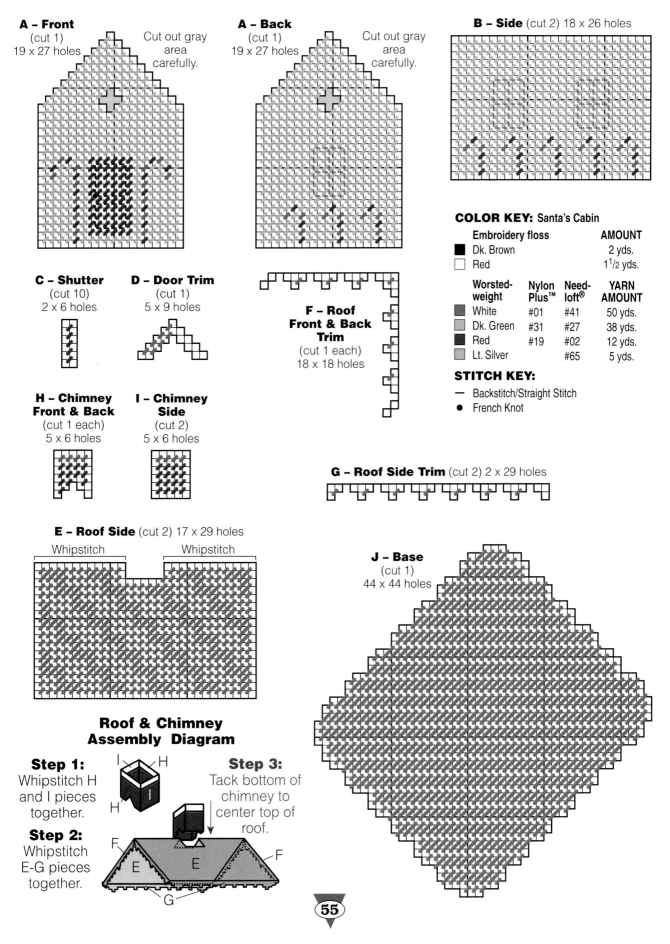

Holiday Gift Bag

Designed by
Michele Wilcox

SIZE: 2½" x 7⅛" x 7⅛" tall, not including handles.

MATERIALS: Two sheets of 7-count plastic canvas; 1 yd. green ½" edging, Worsted-weight or plastic canvas yarn (for amounts see Color Key).

CUTTING INSTRUCTIONS:

A: For sides, cut two according to graph.
B: For ends and bottom, cut three (two for sides and one for bottom) 16 x 46 holes.

STITCHING INSTRUCTIONS:

1: Using colors and stitches indicated, work A and B pieces according to graphs. With dk. red,

Overcast cutout edges of A pieces. With dk. green, Whipstitch A and B pieces together; Overcast unfinished edges.

NOTE: Cut edging in half.

2: For each handle, thread each end of one length of edging from outside to inside through one cutout at top of one A. Knot ends on inside to hold.✧

COLOR KEY: Holiday Gift Bag

	Worsted-weight	Nylon Plus™	Need-loft®	YARN AMOUNT
■	Dk. Red	#20	#01	48 yds.
■	Dk. Green	#31	#27	28 yds.
◩	White	#01	#41	18 yds.
▨	Tangerine	#15	#11	10 yds.

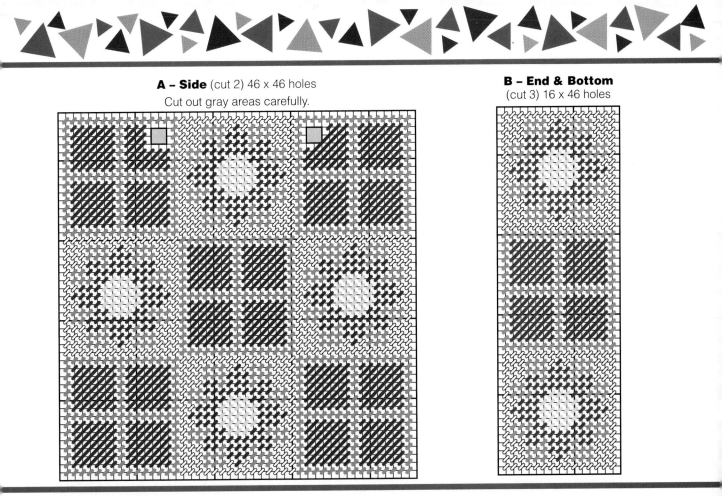

A – Side (cut 2) 46 x 46 holes
Cut out gray areas carefully.

B – End & Bottom
(cut 3) 16 x 46 holes

Glittery Centerpiece

CONTINUED FROM PAGE 53

3: Holding F pieces together and working through both thicknesses as one piece, overlapping three holes to join ends as for ring base side, using white/silver and stitches indicated, work F pieces according to Ring Stitch Pattern Guide on page 53.

4: With white/silver, Whipstitch unfinished edges of ring together. Whipstitch pieces together according to Centerpiece Assembly Diagram. Glue one stone to center of each side as shown in photo.✧

COLOR KEY: Glittery Centerpiece

	Metallic cord	AMOUNT
	White/Silver	35 yds.
	Red/Silver	9 yds.
	White/Gold	9 yds.
	Blue/Silver	5 yds.
	Green/Silver	5 yds.
	Orange/Silver	5 yds.
	Purple/Silver	5 yds.

A – Side

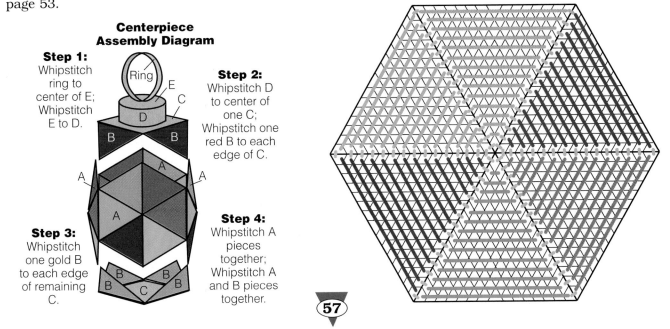

Centerpiece Assembly Diagram

Step 1:
Whipstitch ring to center of E; Whipstitch E to D.

Step 2:
Whipstitch D to center of one C; Whipstitch one red B to each edge of C.

Step 3:
Whipstitch one gold B to each edge of remaining C.

Step 4:
Whipstitch A pieces together; Whipstitch A and B pieces together.

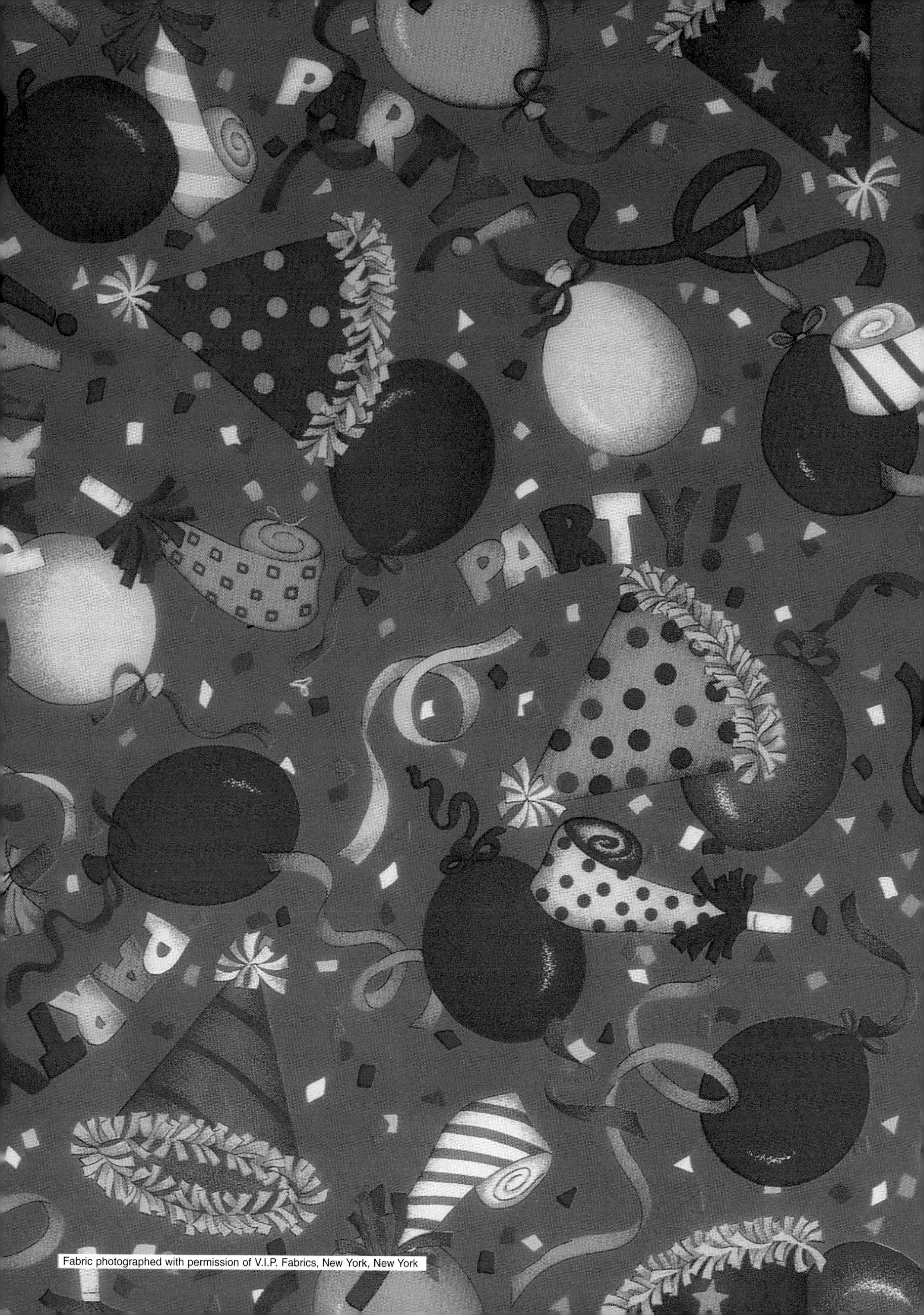

Fabric photographed with permission of V.I.P. Fabrics, New York, New York

Holiday Parties

Whether the party is indoors or out, sharing food and fun with those we love creates memorable moments that make our lives fuller and more joyful. Plan the perfect get-together for family and friends, or add a holiday touch at your next club meeting with hand-stitched party favors, centerpieces, table settings and wall hangings.

Sprinkle stardust across your banquet table with a glittery centerpiece, coasters and ornaments.

Festive Table Decor

Designed by Debby Keel

SIZE: Each Coaster is $4\frac{3}{4}$" x $5\frac{1}{2}$"; Flat Ornament is $4\frac{3}{4}$" x 6"; 3-Dimensional Ornament is $4\frac{1}{2}$" x 6"; Centerpiece is $13\frac{7}{8}$" x $14\frac{1}{2}$".

MATERIALS: Fourteen 5" plastic canvas hexagon shapes; Metallic cord (for amount see Color Key); Worsted-weight or plastic canvas yarn (for amounts see Color Key).

NOTE: For optional Place Mat, purchase 13 hexagons and additional stitching materials. (See Centerpiece Assembly Diagram.)

CUTTING INSTRUCTIONS:

A: Leaving ring at top on two pieces, cut hanging rings off twelve hexagons.

STITCHING INSTRUCTIONS:

1: Using colors and stitches indicated, work two hexagons according to Hexagon Graph; substituting green for red, work two hexagons according to graph. Substituting red and green for white and white for red, work five hexagons (On hexagon with hanging ring, work background in green and star in white.) in each color combination according to graph.

2: For Coasters, with cord, Overcast one of each white hexagon and one red hexagon. For Flat Ornament, Overcast green hexagon with hanging ring.

3: For 3-Dimensional Ornament, holding pieces wrong sides together, with cord, Whipstitch one white with green center, one green and one red hexagon (with hanging ring) together; Overcast hanging ring.

4: For Centerpiece, with cord, Whipstitch remaining pieces together according to Centerpiece Assembly Diagram; Overcast unfinished edges.✧

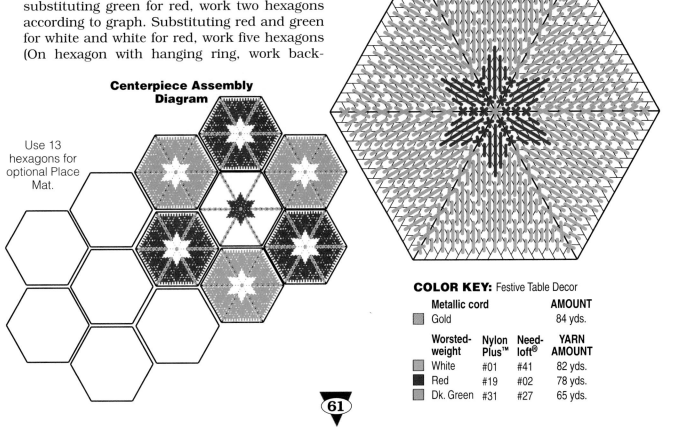

Hexagon Graph

Centerpiece Assembly Diagram

Use 13 hexagons for optional Place Mat.

COLOR KEY: Festive Table Decor

Metallic cord			AMOUNT
Gold			84 yds.

Worsted-weight	Nylon Plus™	Need-loft®	YARN AMOUNT
White	#01	#41	82 yds.
Red	#19	#02	78 yds.
Dk. Green	#31	#27	65 yds.

Halloween Mini Baskets

Designed by
Cherie Marie Leck

SIZE: Each is 2" x 3" x 4¼", including handle.

MATERIALS: One sheet of 7-count plastic canvas; Craft glue or glue gun; Worsted-weight or plastic canvas yarn (for amounts see Color Key).

CUTTING INSTRUCTIONS:

A: For sides, cut six 13 x 19 holes.
B: For ends, cut six 13 x 13 holes.
C: For bottoms, cut three 13 x 19 holes (no graph).
D: For handles and linings, cut six (three for handles and three for linings) 4 x 37 holes.
E: For bat, cut one according to graph.
F: For ghost, cut one according to graph.
G: For pumpkin, cut one according to graph.

STITCHING INSTRUCTIONS:

NOTE: C and lining D pieces are unworked.

1: Using colors and stitches indicated, work A, B, three D pieces for handles, F and G pieces according to graphs. Using black and Continental Stitch, work E. With purple for bat, black for ghost and cinnamon and dk. green for pumpkin (see photo), Overcast edges of E-G pieces.

2: Using colors indicated, Backstitch, French Knot and Straight Stitch, embroider facial detail as indicated on E and F graphs.

3: For each handle, holding unworked D to wrong side of one worked piece, with white and dk. orange (alternate colors as shown in photo), Whipstitch long edges together. For each Basket, with dk. orange, Whipstitch two A, two B and one C piece together according to Basket Assembly Diagram; with alternating white and dk. orange, Overcast unfinished edges, catching ends of one handle on opposite ends to join as indicated (see diagram) as you work.

4: Tie remaining dk. orange into a bow; trim ends. Glue bow to ghost and bat, ghost and pumpkin to Baskets as shown.✧

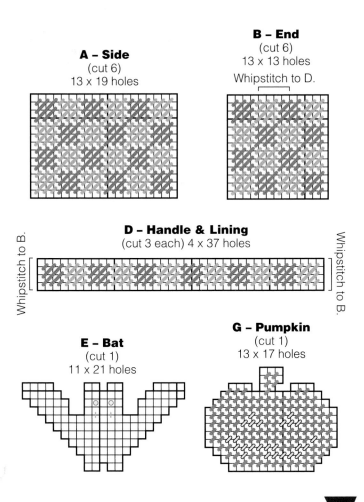

A – Side
(cut 6)
13 x 19 holes

B – End
(cut 6)
13 x 13 holes
Whipstitch to D.

D – Handle & Lining
(cut 3 each) 4 x 37 holes
Whipstitch to B. | Whipstitch to B.

E – Bat
(cut 1)
11 x 21 holes

G – Pumpkin
(cut 1)
13 x 17 holes

COLOR KEY: Halloween Mini Baskets

	Worsted-weight	Nylon Plus™	Need-loft®	YARN AMOUNT
▨	Dk. Orange	#18	#52	45 yds.
▨	White	#01	#41	40 yds.
■	Black	#02	#00	5 yds.
☐	Purple	#21	#46	2 yds.
▨	Yellow	#26	#57	2 yds.
☐	Cinnamon	#44	#14	1 yd.
▨	Dk. Green	#31	#27	1 yd.

STITCH KEY:

— Backstitch/Straight Stitch
● French Knot

F – Ghost
(cut 1)
12 x 16 holes

Basket Assembly Diagram

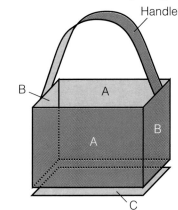

Handle

B · A

A · B

C

Shamrock Welcome

Designed by Trudy Bath Smith

SIZE: 46" long, not including ties.

MATERIALS: Four sheets of 7-count plastic canvas; Craft glue or glue gun; Metallic cord (for amounts see Color Key on page 66); Raffia straw (for amount see Color Key); Worsted-weight or plastic canvas yarn (for amounts see Color Key).

CUTTING INSTRUCTIONS:

NOTE: Graphs on page 66.

A: For shamrocks, cut five according to graph.

B: For faces, cut four according to graph.

C: For noses, cut four according to graph.

D: For bodies, cut four according to graph:

E: For arms, cut four according to graph.

F: For legs, cut four according to graph.

G: For letters, cut number needed according to graphs.

Post your wee leprechaun friends with a smilin' Irish greeting.

STITCHING INSTRUCTIONS:

1: Using colors and stitches indicated, work A, B and D-G pieces according to graphs. With flesh for nose, black/green cord for shamrocks, gold cord for letters and with matching colors, Overcast edges of A and C-G pieces.

2: Using colors indicated, Backstitch, French Knot and Fly Stitch, embroider facial detail as indicated on B graph.

3: Using dk. orange and Looped Overcast (leave 2" loops), Overcast edges of B as indicated; cut loops and fray yarn to fluff. With flesh, Overcast unfinished edges.

4: For each leprechaun, glue one each B-F piece together as shown in photo. Alternating motifs, glue shamrocks and leprechauns together (see photo); glue letters to Garland as shown.

NOTE: Cut one 90" length of black/green cord.

5: For hanger, leaving 30" of cord hanging on each side, glue 90" black/green cord to wrong side along entire length of Garland.✧

Shamrock Welcome

PHOTO ON PAGES 64 & 65

A – Shamrock
(cut 5)
33 x 33 holes

B – Face
(cut 4) 18 x 18 holes

Overcast with dk. orange.

Overcast with dk. orange.

D – Body
(cut 4)
22 x 22 holes

C – Nose
(cut 4)
2 x 2 holes

F – Legs
(cut 4)
26 x 26 holes

E – Arms
(cut 4)
29 x 29 holes

G – Letter "W"
(cut 1)
13 x 15 holes

G – Letter "E"
(cut 2)
9 x 15 holes

G – Letter "L"
(cut 1)
9 x 15 holes

G – Letter "C"
(cut 1)
9 x 15 holes

G – Letter "O"
(cut 1)
9 x 15 holes

Cut Out

G – Letter "M"
(cut 1)
13 x 15 holes

COLOR KEY: Shamrock Welcome

Metallic cord			AMOUNT
■ Black/Green			25 yds.
White/Gold			10 yds.
□ Gold			7 yds.
Raffia			**AMOUNT**
Dk. Green			50 yds.

Worsted-weight	Nylon Plus™	Need-loft®	YARN AMOUNT
Green	#58	#28	45 yds.
Dk. Orange	#18	#52	30 yds.
Flesh	#14	#56	18 yds.
Forest	#32	#29	12 yds.
Rose	#12	#05	4 yds.
Black	#02	#00	2 yds.

STITCH KEY:

— Backstitch/Straight Stitch
● French Knot
▲ Nose Placement
Ψ Fly Stitch

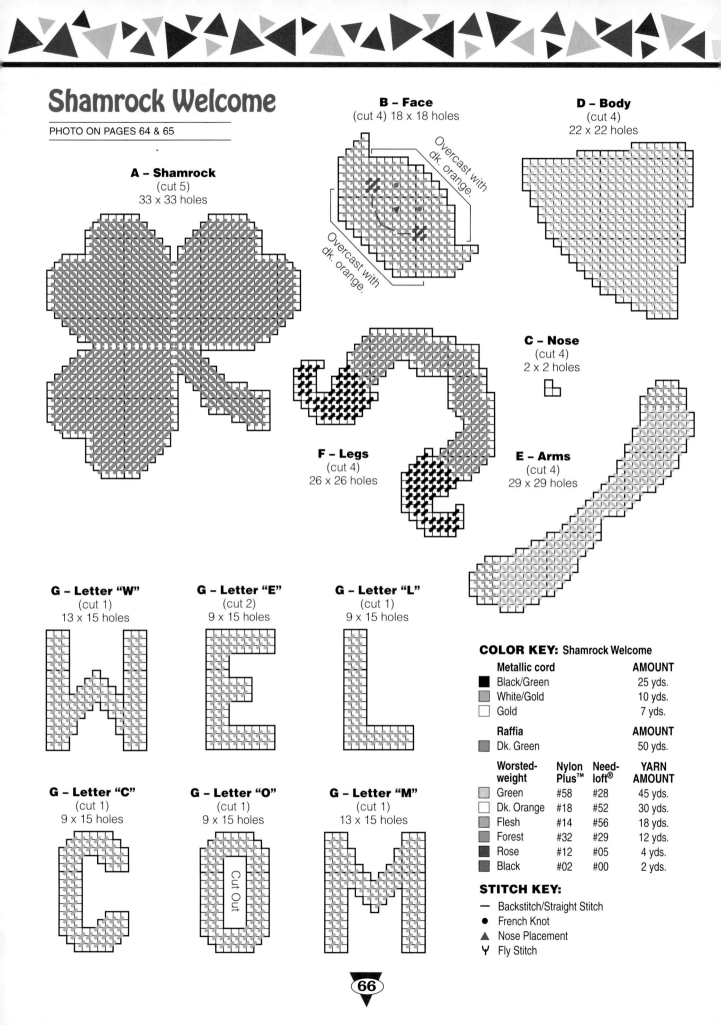

New Year Hats

Designed by Robin Will

SIZE: Each Hat is 9½" x 9¾" x 5¼" tall; each Headband is 1⅛" x 5½" across x 9".

MATERIALS: 14 sheets of 7-count plastic canvas; 49 assorted-color 8-mm round acrylic faceted stones; Two ⅜" plastic headbands; 1 yd. black elastic cord; Craft glue or glue gun; Six-strand embroidery floss (for amount see Color Key on page 69); Metallic cord (for amount see Color Key); Worsted-weight or plastic canvas yarn (for amounts see Color Key).

CUTTING INSTRUCTIONS:

NOTE: Graphs on pages 68 & 69.

A: For hat brim tops and linings, cut four (two for tops and two for linings) according to graph.

B: For hat side pieces, cut four 31 x 67 holes (no graph).

C: For hat tops, cut two according to graph.

D: For hatband backs, cut two 5 x 69 holes (no graph).

E: For hatband front #1, cut one according to graph.

F: For hatband front #2, cut one according to graph.

G: For headband cover pieces, cut four according to graph.

H: For headband top #1, cut two according to graph.

I: For headband top #2, cut two according to graph.

STITCHING INSTRUCTIONS:

NOTE: Two G pieces are unworked.

1: Using black and white and Continental Stitch, work two A and one D piece in each color. Using black and white and Slanted Gobelin Stitch over three bars, work two B pieces in each color in horizontal rows across

New Year Hats

CONTINUED FROM PAGE 67

length of pieces.

2: Using black and Slanted Gobelin Stitch, work one C according to graph; substituting white for black, work remaining C according to graph.

3: Using colors and stitches indicated, work E, F, one G, H and I pieces according to graphs; substituting white for black, work one G according to graph.

4: Using six strands floss and metallic cord, Backstitch, Straight Stitch and French Knot, embroider detail on E, F and one of each H and I pieces as indicated on graphs; continuing embroidery pattern established on hatband fronts, using cord and Straight Stitch, embroider detail on D pieces.

5: For each Hat, with matching color yarn,

Whipstitch matching color A-C pieces together according to Hat Assembly Diagram. For hatband #1, with black, Whipstitch ends of E and black D together; Overcast unfinished edges. For hat band #2, with white, repeat as above with F and white D.

6: For headband #1, holding one unworked G to wrong side of white G with one plastic headband between, with white, Whipstitch together. Holding H pieces wrong sides together, Whipstitch together as indicated; Overcast unfinished edges. For headband #2, with black, repeat as above with remaining G and I pieces.

NOTE: Cut elastic cord in half.

7: For each chin strap, assemble one Hat and one elastic cord according to Chin Strap Assembly Diagram.

8: Glue stones to hatbands and headband tops (see photo); glue hatbands to Hats and headband tops to Headbands as shown.✧

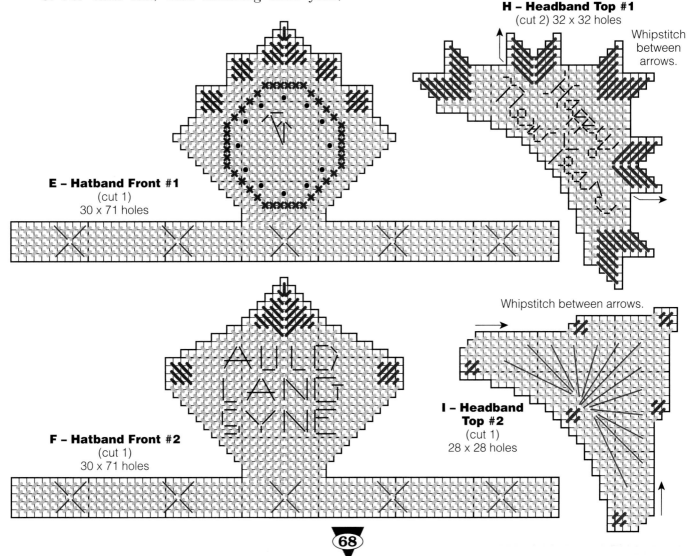

E – Hatband Front #1
(cut 1)
30 x 71 holes

F – Hatband Front #2
(cut 1)
30 x 71 holes

H – Headband Top #1
(cut 2) 32 x 32 holes

Whipstitch between arrows.

Whipstitch between arrows.

I – Headband Top #2
(cut 1)
28 x 28 holes

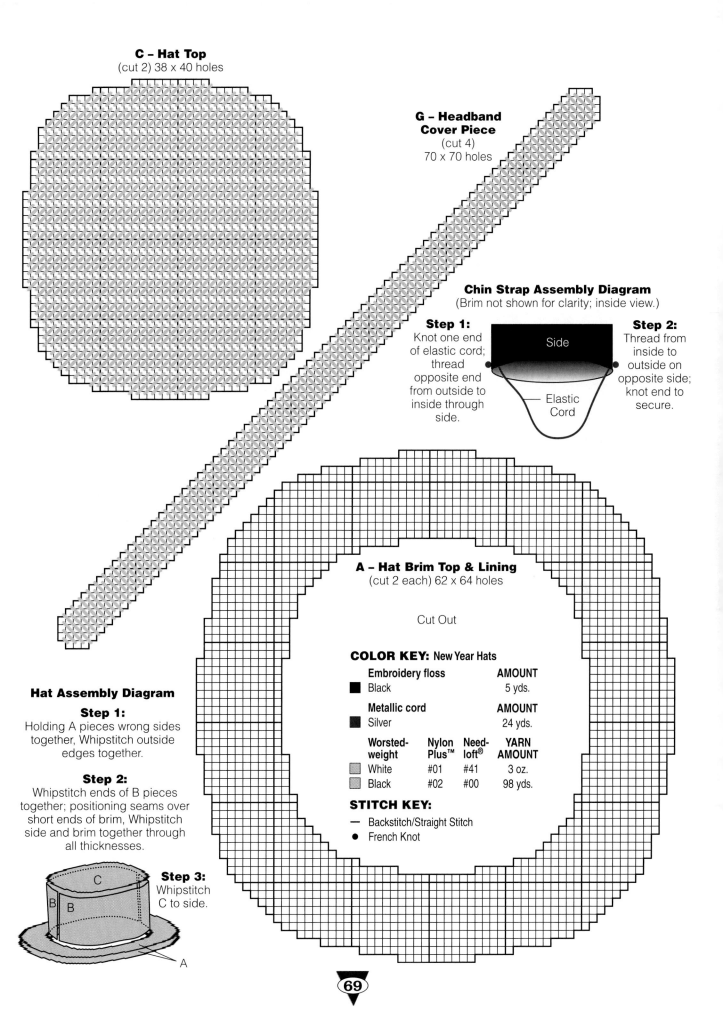

C – Hat Top
(cut 2) 38 x 40 holes

G – Headband Cover Piece
(cut 4)
70 x 70 holes

Chin Strap Assembly Diagram
(Brim not shown for clarity; inside view.)

Step 1:
Knot one end of elastic cord; thread opposite end from outside to inside through side.

Side

Step 2:
Thread from inside to outside on opposite side; knot end to secure.

Elastic Cord

A – Hat Brim Top & Lining
(cut 2 each) 62 x 64 holes

Cut Out

COLOR KEY: New Year Hats

Embroidery floss				AMOUNT
■ Black				5 yds.

Metallic cord				AMOUNT
■ Silver				24 yds.

	Worsted-weight	Nylon Plus™	Need-loft®	YARN AMOUNT
▨	White	#01	#41	3 oz.
▨	Black	#02	#00	98 yds.

STITCH KEY:
— Backstitch/Straight Stitch
● French Knot

Hat Assembly Diagram

Step 1:
Holding A pieces wrong sides together, Whipstitch outside edges together.

Step 2:
Whipstitch ends of B pieces together; positioning seams over short ends of brim, Whipstitch side and brim together through all thicknesses.

Step 3:
Whipstitch C to side.

Pack these tiny party favor bags full of sweets, and send a heartfelt message to your favorite valentines.

Valentine Bags

Designed by Mary T. Cosgrove

SIZE: Each is 1½" x 3½" x 4¾" tall, not including handle.

MATERIALS: 1½ sheets of red 7-count plastic canvas; ½ sheet of white 7-count plastic canvas; Worsted-weight or plastic canvas yarn (for amounts see Color Key).

CUTTING INSTRUCTIONS:

A: For Bag sides, cut six from red 22 x 30 holes.

B: For Bag ends, cut six from red 10 x 30 holes (no graph).

C: For Bag bottoms, cut three from red 10 x 22 holes (no graph).

D: For Bag handles, cut three from red 3 x 40 holes (no graph).

E: For "Love" signs, cut two from white 10 x 22 holes.

F: For large heart signs, cut four from white 6 x 22 holes.

G: For small heart signs, cut two from white 10 x 22 holes.

STITCHING INSTRUCTIONS:

NOTE: B-D pieces are unworked.

1: For each "Love" side (make two), positioning one E on one A as indicated on graph, using colors and stitches indicated, work through both thicknesses as one piece according to Love Graph.

2: For each large heart side (make two), positioning two F pieces on one A as indicated, using colors and stitches indicated, work through both thicknesses as one piece according to Large Hearts Graph.

3: For each small heart side (make two), positioning one G on one A as indicated, using colors and stitches indicated, work through both thicknesses as one piece according to Small Hearts Graph.

4: For each Bag, with white, Whipstitch matching A, two B, one C and one D piece together according to Bag Assembly Diagram; Overcast unfinished edges.✧

COLOR KEY: Valentine Bags

	Worsted-weight	Nylon Plus™	Need-loft®	YARN AMOUNT
White	#01	#41	21 yds.
Red	#19	#02	11 yds.

STITCH KEY:
- ☐ Sign Attachment

Love Graph   **Large Hearts Graph**   **Small Hearts Graph**

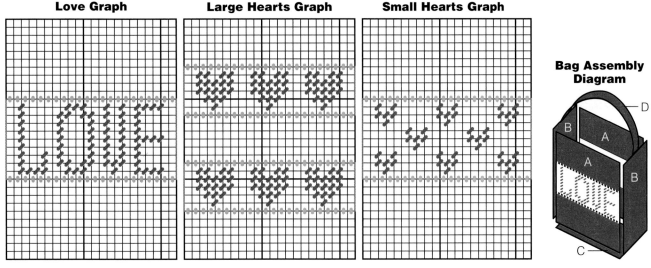

Bag Assembly Diagram

LET FREEDOM RING

Celebrate Independence Day with stars & stripes windchimes and a backyard barbecue.

Let Freedom Ring

Designed by
Robin Will

Instructions on page 75

July 4th Picnic

Designed by Nancy Marshall

SIZE: Basket is 4⅞" x 9⅛" x 9⅛" tall; Napkin Ring is 2" x 3⅝" x 4⅛".

MATERIALS: 2½ sheets of 7-count plastic canvas; Three blue 9" x 12" sheets of felt; Craft glue or glue gun; Worsted-weight or plastic canvas yarn (for amounts see Color Key on page 75).

CUTTING INSTRUCTIONS:

NOTE: Graphs on pages 74 & 75.

A: For Basket sides, cut two according to graph.

B: For Basket ends, cut two 24 x 31 holes.

C: For Basket bottom, cut one 31 x 59 holes (no graph).

D: For Basket handle, cut one 11 x 69 holes.

E: For Basket and Napkin Ring bow loops, cut three (two for Basket and one for Napkin Ring) 7 x 57 holes.

F: For Basket and Napkin Ring bow centers, cut three (two for Basket and one for Napkin Ring) 7 x 19 holes.

G: For Basket and Napkin Ring bow tails, cut six (two for each bow) 6 x 18 holes.

H: For Napkin Ring band, cut one 7 x 34 holes (no graph).

I: For Basket linings, using A-D pieces as patterns, cut one each from felt ⅛" smaller at all edges.

STITCHING INSTRUCTIONS:

NOTE: C piece is unworked.

1: Using colors and stitches indicated, work A, B and D-G (leave indicated and uncoded areas on E pieces unworked) pieces according to graphs; using royal and Continental Stitch work H.

2: For Napkin Ring band, with royal,

July 4th Picnic

CONTINUED FROM PAGE 73

Whipstitch ends of H together. With matching colors as shown in photo, Overcast edges of F-H pieces.

3: For Basket, with matching colors, Whipstitch A-D pieces together as indicated; with royal, Overcast edges. Glue I pieces to inside of Basket and underside of handle.

4: For each bow, Whipstitch and assemble one E, one F and two G pieces as indicated and according to Bow Assembly Diagram. Glue one bow to each side of Basket and remaining bow to Napkin Ring band as shown.✧

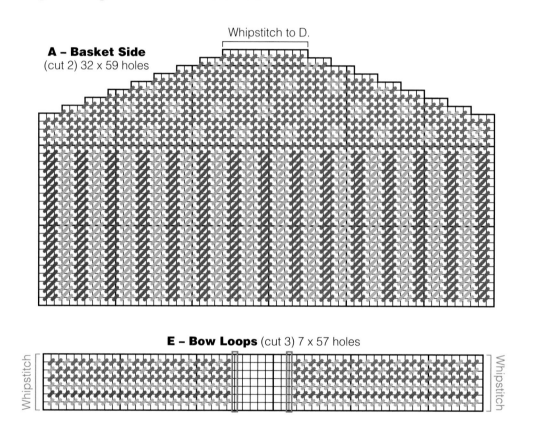

Whipstitch to D.

A – Basket Side
(cut 2) 32 x 59 holes

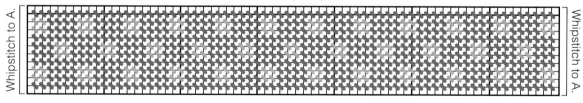

E – Bow Loops (cut 3) 7 x 57 holes

Whipstitch

Whipstitch

D – Basket Handle (cut 1) 11 x 69 holes

Whipstitch to A.

Whipstitch to A.

Bow Assembly Diagram

Step 1:
With royal, Whipstitch ends of E to indicated bars at center; with matching colors as shown in photo, Overcast edges of loops.

E

Step 2:
Wrap F around center of E, overlapping and gluing ends together and to back of loops to secure.

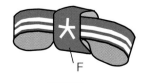

F

Step 3:
Glue G pieces together; glue to back of bow.

G

B – Basket End (cut 2) 24 x 31 holes

F – Bow Center
(cut 3)
7 x 19 holes

G – Bow Tail
(cut 6)
6 x 18 holes

COLOR KEY: July 4th Picnic

Worsted-weight	Nylon Plus™	Need-loft®	YARN AMOUNT
■ Royal	#09	#32	50 yds.
■ Red	#19	#02	42 yds.
▨ White	#01	#41	42 yds.

STITCH KEY:
□ Unworked Area/Loop End Attachment

Let Freedom Ring

PHOTO ON PAGE 72

SIZE: 10¼" x about 29" long, including hanger.

MATERIALS: Two sheets of 7-count plastic canvas; Eight gold 1⅛" liberty bells; 1 yd. each of red and blue ¼" picot-edged satin ribbon; 5 yds. ⅛" jute; Polyester fiberfill; Craft glue or glue gun; Worsted-weight or plastic canvas yarn (for amounts see Color Key on page 76).

CUTTING INSTRUCTIONS:

NOTE: Graphs on page 76.

A: For banner, cut two according to graph.
B: For stars, cut twelve according to graph.

STITCHING INSTRUCTIONS:

1: Using colors and stitches indicated, work A pieces according to graph; fill in uncoded areas using white and Continental Stitch. Using red and royal and Continental Stitch, work six B pieces in each color.

NOTE: Cut jute into one 40", two 30" and two 20" lengths for chimes; cut one 30" length for hanger.

2: For each bell chime, thread one bell onto center of one chimes jute strand, fold strand in half at bell and knot above bell. Knot ends together at opposite end. To attach each star, holding two matching color B pieces wrong sides together with bell chime between (see Chimes Assembly Diagram), with white, Whipstitch together.

3: For hanger, fold 30" strand in half; knot each end and a tie a loop knot in center (see photo).

4: For banner, holding A pieces wrong sides together with knotted ends of hanger and chimes between as indicated on A graph, with white, Whipstitch together (see diagram), stuffing with fiberfill before closing.

NOTE: Cut each color ribbon into three equal lengths.

5: For each bow, holding one of each color ribbon together, thread one bell onto center of ribbons; tie ribbons into a bow and trim ends. Glue bows to banner as shown in photo.✧

Let Freedom Ring

PHOTO ON PAGE 72

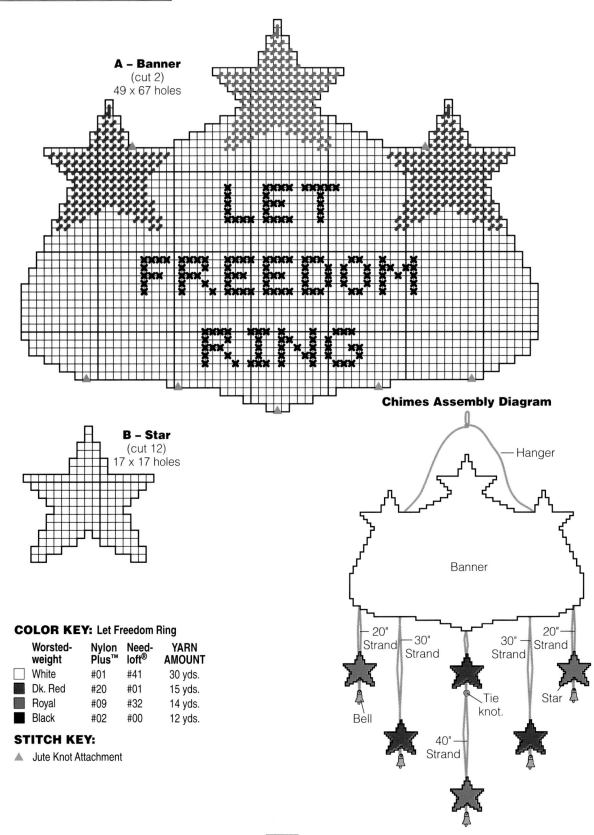

A – Banner
(cut 2)
49 x 67 holes

B – Star
(cut 12)
17 x 17 holes

Chimes Assembly Diagram

Hanger

Banner

20"
Strand

30"
Strand

30"
Strand

20"
Strand

Star

Tie
knot.

Bell

40"
Strand

COLOR KEY: Let Freedom Ring

	Worsted-weight	Nylon Plus™	Need-loft®	YARN AMOUNT
☐	White	#01	#41	30 yds.
■	Dk. Red	#20	#01	15 yds.
■	Royal	#09	#32	14 yds.
■	Black	#02	#00	12 yds.

STITCH KEY:

▲ Jute Knot Attachment

Love Note Magnets

Designed by Stephen E. Reedy

SIZE: Each is 2" x 2".

MATERIALS FOR ONE: Scrap of 10-count plastic canvas; Magnetic strip; Craft glue or glue gun; Six-strand embroidery floss (for amount see Color Key on page 79); Sport-weight yarn (for amount see Color Key).

CUTTING INSTRUCTIONS:

A: For heart, cut one according to graph on page 79.

STITCHING INSTRUCTIONS:

1: Using yarn and stitches indicated, work A according to graph; Overcast edges. Using three strands floss and Backstitch, embroider message of choice (center on heart) according to Letter Graph on page 79.

2: Glue magnetic strip to back.✧

Pilgrim Coasters

Designed by Dorothy Tabor

SIZE: Each Coaster is 4⅜" x 5⅜"; Holder is 1⅝" x 4⅜" x 5⅜" tall.

MATERIALS: Two sheets of 7-count plastic canvas; Six-strand embroidery floss (for amounts see Color Key); Worsted-weight or plastic canvas yarn (for amounts see Color Key).

CUTTING INSTRUCTIONS:

A: For Coasters and Holder front, cut five (four for Coasters and one for Holder front) according to graph.

B: For Holder back, cut one according to graph.

C: For Holder bottom, cut one 10 x 27 holes (no graph).

D: For Holder ends, cut two 3 x 10 holes (no graph).

STITCHING INSTRUCTIONS:

NOTE: C piece is unworked.

1: Using colors and stitches indicated, work one A for Holder front, remaining A pieces for Coasters and B piece according to graphs. Using silver and gray and Continental Stitch, work one D in each color. With matching colors as shown in photo, Overcast Coaster A pieces.

2: Using six strands floss in colors indicated, Backstitch, Straight Stitch and French Knot, embroider detail as indicated on graphs.

3: With matching colors, Whipstitch Holder Front A, and B-D pieces together as indicated and according to Holder Assembly Diagram; Overcast unfinished edges. ✧

A – Coaster & Holder Front
(cut 5) 28 x 35 holes

B – Holder Back
(cut 1) 28 x 35 holes

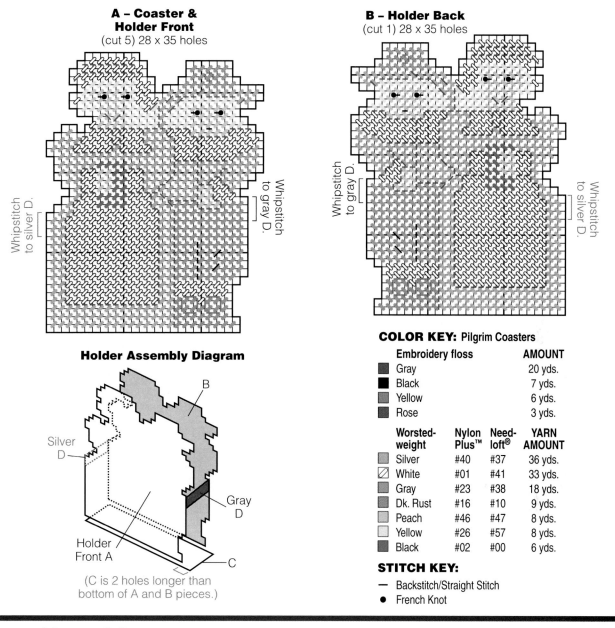

Whipstitch to silver D.

Whipstitch to gray D.

Whipstitch to gray D.

Whipstitch to silver D.

Holder Assembly Diagram

B

Silver D

Gray D

Holder Front A

C

(C is 2 holes longer than bottom of A and B pieces.)

COLOR KEY: Pilgrim Coasters

Embroidery floss			AMOUNT
Gray			20 yds.
Black			7 yds.
Yellow			6 yds.
Rose			3 yds.

Worsted-weight	Nylon Plus™	Need-loft®	YARN AMOUNT
Silver	#40	#37	36 yds.
White	#01	#41	33 yds.
Gray	#23	#38	18 yds.
Dk. Rust	#16	#10	9 yds.
Peach	#46	#47	8 yds.
Yellow	#26	#57	8 yds.
Black	#02	#00	6 yds.

STITCH KEY:
— Backstitch/Straight Stitch
● French Knot

Love Note Magnets

PHOTO ON PAGE 77

A – Heart
(cut 1)
19 x 19 holes

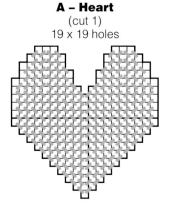

Letter Graph

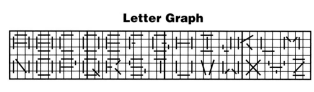

COLOR KEY: Love Note Magnets

Embroidery floss	AMOUNT
Black	1-2 yds.

Sport-weight	YARN AMOUNT
Color of Choice	5 yds.

STITCH KEY:
— Backstitch/Straight Stitch

Easter Treats

Emerging from
a dark winter's sleep,
branches fill with singing
birds, and wildflowers appear
in the fields. Spring blooms with a
fragrant sense of renewal and vitality.
Now is the time to try something new ...
Involve your church group in a
stitching circle to create devotional
gifts, or let the kids help
glue the finishing
touches on your
next spring
project.

Plant sweet flowers and find a cheery bunny on your new garden-fresh tissue cover.

Easter Surprises

Designed by Nancy W. Dorman

SIZE: Snugly covers a boutique-style tissue box.

MATERIALS: 1¼ sheets of 7-count plastic canvas; One sheet of 10-count plastic canvas; Craft glue or glue gun; Six-strand embroidery floss (for amounts see Color Key on page 84); Worsted-weight or plastic canvas yarn (for amounts see Color Key).

CUTTING INSTRUCTIONS:

NOTES: Graphs o npage 84. Use 7-count for A and B and 10-count canvas for remaining pieces.

A: For Cover sides, cut four 29 x 37 holes.

B: For Cover top, cut one according to graph.

C: For bunnies, cut two according to graph.

D: For egg upper and lower pieces, cut two each according to graphs.

E: For letters, cut number needed according to graphs.

F: For large flower petals, cut two according to graph.

G: For small flower petals, cut eight according to graph.

STITCHING INSTRUCTIONS:

1: Using colors and stitches indicated, work A and B pieces according to graphs. Using six strands purple floss and Backstitch, embroider outlines as indicated on A and B graphs.

2: Using white and Herringbone Overcast, Overcast cutout edges of B. Using white and Herringbone Whipstitch, Whipstitch A and B pieces together, forming Cover; using Herringbone Overcast, Overcast unfinished edges.

NOTE: Separate remaining yarn into 2-ply or nylon plastic canvas into 1-ply strands; use 2-ply (or 1-ply) strands throughout.

3: Using colors and stitches indicated, work C-G pieces according to graphs; fill in uncoded areas of C and D pieces using white and Continental Stitch. With white for bunnies and with matching colors, Overcast edges of C and D pieces.

4: With yarn colors shown in photo or in desired color combinations for letters, white for large flower petals and four small flower petals and pink for remaining small flower petals, Overcast edges of E-G pieces.

5: Using yarn and six strands floss in colors indicated (use pink for white flower centers and white for pink flower centers), Backstitch, Straight Stitch and French Knot, embroider egg detail, bunny facial features and flower centers as indicated on C, D, F and G graphs.

6: With matching colors, tack letters and flowers to two opposite Cover sides as indicated and bunnies and egg pieces to remaining cover sides as shown in photo. Using lt. green and Straight Stitch, embroider leaves and stems on Cover sides with flowers as indicated on A graph; if desired, embroider grass blades on remaining Cover sides (see photo) through all thicknesses.

7: Cut remaining red floss in half; tie each length into a bow and trim ends. Glue one bow to each bunny as shown.✧

Easter Surprises

PHOTO ON PAGE 82

B – Cover Top
(cut 1) 29 x 29 holes

Cut Out

A – Cover Side
(cut 4) 29 x 37 holes

E – Letter "E"
(cut 4 from 10-count)
4 x 7 holes

E – Letter "A"
(cut 4 from 10-count)
4 x 7 holes

Cut Out

E – Letter "S"
(cut 2 from 10-count)
4 x 7 holes

COLOR KEY: Easter Surprises

Embroidery floss			AMOUNT
■ Purple			8 yds.
■ Red			4 yds.

Worsted-weight	Nylon Plus™	Need-loft®	YARN AMOUNT
Lavender	#22	#45	40 yds.
White	#01	#41	36 yds.
Pink	#11	#07	5 yds.
Lt. Green	#28	#26	4 yds.
Lt. Blue	#05	#36	2 yds.
Lt. Yellow	#42	#21	2 yds.
Peach	#46	#47	2 yds.
■ Letter or Flower Color of Choice			

STITCH KEY:
— Backstitch/Straight Stitch
● French Knot
□ Letter Attachment
□ Flower Attachments

E – Letter "H"
(cut 2 from 10-count)
4 x 7 holes

E – Letter "P"
(cut 4 from 10-count)
4 x 7 holes

Cut Out

E – Letter "Y"
(cut 2 from 10-count)
5 x 7 holes

E – Letter "T"
(cut 2 from 10-count)
5 x 7 holes

C – Bunny
(cut 2 from 10-count) 21 x 24 holes

F – Large Flower Petals
(cut 2 from 10-count)
5 x 5 holes

E – Letter "R"
(cut 2 from 10-count)
4 x 7 holes

Cut Out

D – Egg Upper Piece
(cut 2 from 10-count) 21 x 30 holes

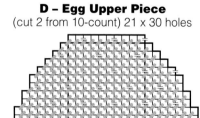

G – Small Flower Petals
(cut 8 from 10-count)
3 x 3 holes

D – Egg Lower Piece
(cut 2 from 10-count) 16 x 30 holes

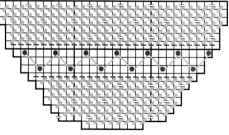

Bright 'n' Bold

Designed by Diane T. Ray

*Instructions
on next page*

Bright 'n' Bold

PHOTO ON PAGE 85

SIZE: 7½" across x 3½" tall, not including handle.

MATERIALS: One sheet of white 12" x 18" or larger 7-count plastic canvas; ¾ sheet of neon pink and ½ sheet (90 holes long) each of neon blue, neon lime and neon purple 7-count plastic canvas; One 9½" plastic canvas radial circle; Worsted-weight or plastic canvas yarn (for amounts see Color Key).

CUTTING INSTRUCTIONS:

A: For side pieces, cut two from white according to graph.

B: For handle base, cut one from white according to graph.

C: For bottom, cut away outer seven rows of holes from canvas circle to measure 7⅜" across (no graph).

D: For bow loops, cut one from pink according to graph.

E: For bow center, cut one from purple according to graph.

F: For handle overlay strips, cut one from green and one from blue 3 x 77 holes (no graph).

G: For long weaving strips, cut four from pink and two from purple 3 x 89 holes (no graph).

H: For short weaving strips, cut fourteen from blue and fourteen from green 3 x 19 holes (no graph).

I: For weaving laces, cut number of straight bars needed from purple, 90 holes long (no graph).

STITCHING INSTRUCTIONS:

NOTE: Pieces are unworked.

1: Overlapping ends of A pieces as indicated on graph and weaving through both thicknesses as one, weave G pieces horizontally (hide ends under side spokes) through cutouts on A pieces according to Basket Assembly Diagram.

2: Holding F pieces to B as indicated on B graph, weave I pieces through both thicknesses according to graph, forming handle; with matching yarn colors, Whipstitch ends of B to F pieces. Leaving ends of B facing inside, weave ends of handle vertically through cutouts on opposite sides of Basket according to diagram; weave H pieces vertically through remaining cutouts according to diagram.

3: Weave I pieces around Basket as indicated and according to diagram. With white, Whipstitch Basket side and ends of F and H pieces to C through all thicknesses.

4: With bt. pink, Whipstitch ends of D together as indicated; hold center of D and seam together, forming bow loops. Holding D to center top of handle and E to center of D, with bt. purple, tack together through all thicknesses. ✧

Basket Assembly Diagram
(Small section of side shown at overlap and handle attachment areas.)

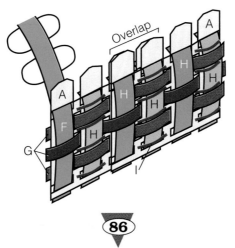

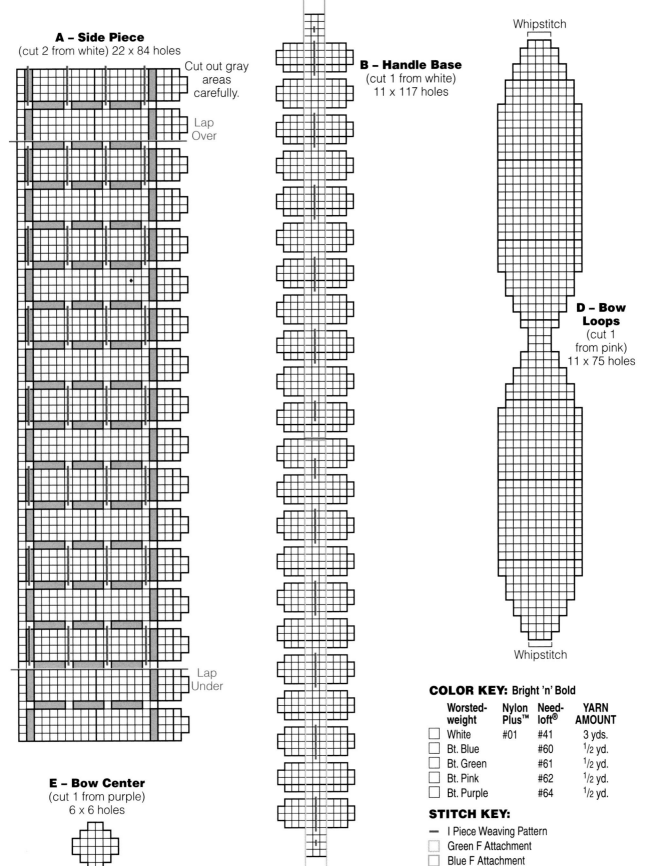

A – Side Piece
(cut 2 from white) 22 x 84 holes

Cut out gray areas carefully.

Lap Over

B – Handle Base
(cut 1 from white)
11 x 117 holes

Whipstitch

D – Bow Loops
(cut 1 from pink)
11 x 75 holes

Lap Under

Whipstitch

E – Bow Center
(cut 1 from purple)
6 x 6 holes

COLOR KEY: Bright 'n' Bold

	Worsted-weight	Nylon Plus™	Need-loft®	YARN AMOUNT
☐	White	#01	#41	3 yds.
☐	Bt. Blue		#60	1/2 yd.
☐	Bt. Green		#61	1/2 yd.
☐	Bt. Pink		#62	1/2 yd.
☐	Bt. Purple		#64	1/2 yd.

STITCH KEY:

— I Piece Weaving Pattern
☐ Green F Attachment
☐ Blue F Attachment

Bunny Hop

Designed by
Dorothy Tabor

SIZE: Each Coaster is 4⅝" x 4⅝"; Holder is 2½" x 5" x 4" tall.

MATERIALS: Two sheets of 7-count plastic canvas; Craft glue or glue gun; Six-strand embroidery floss (for amount see Color Key); Worsted-weight or plastic canvas yarn (for amounts see Color Key).

CUTTING INSTRUCTIONS:

A: For Coasters, cut four according to graph.

B: For Holder front, cut one according to graph.

C: For Holder back, cut one according to graph.

D: For Holder sides, cut two according to graph.

E: For Holder bottom, cut one according to graph.

F: For tulips, cut one according to graph.

G: For eggs #1-#3, cut one each according to graphs.

STITCHING INSTRUCTIONS:

1: Using colors and stitches indicated, work A, E (leave indicated area unworked), F and G pieces according to graphs; fill in uncoded areas of A and work B-D (one D on opposite side of canvas) pieces using white and Continental Stitch.

2: With matching colors, Overcast edges of A pieces. With pink, Overcast cutout edges of B-D pieces. With yellow for egg #1, sea green for egg #2 and watermelon for egg #3, Overcast edges of G pieces. With yellow for petals and with dk. green, Overcast edges of F as indi-

cated on graph.

3: Using six strands floss and Backstitch, embroider facial features and outlines as indicated on A graph.

4: Whipstitch B-E pieces together as indicated and according to Holder Assembly Diagram. With dk. green, Whipstitch F to right side of E as indicated; Overcast unfinished edges of E. Glue eggs to Holder front (see photo).✧

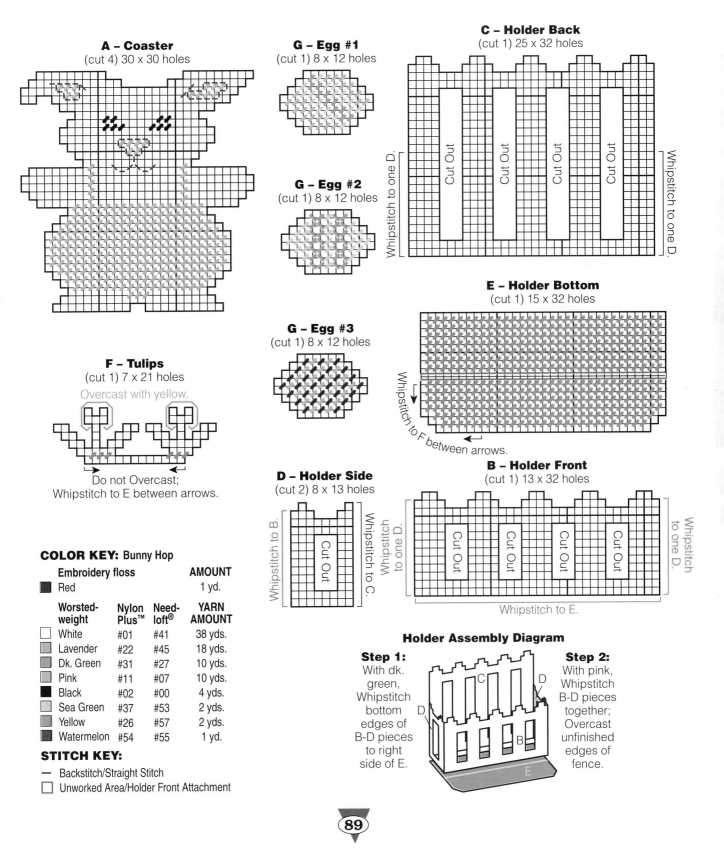

A – Coaster
(cut 4) 30 x 30 holes

G – Egg #1
(cut 1) 8 x 12 holes

G – Egg #2
(cut 1) 8 x 12 holes

G – Egg #3
(cut 1) 8 x 12 holes

C – Holder Back
(cut 1) 25 x 32 holes

Whipstitch to one D.

Cut Out

Whipstitch to one D.

E – Holder Bottom
(cut 1) 15 x 32 holes

Whipstitch to F between arrows.

F – Tulips
(cut 1) 7 x 21 holes

Overcast with yellow.

Do not Overcast;
Whipstitch to E between arrows.

D – Holder Side
(cut 2) 8 x 13 holes

Whipstitch to B.
Cut Out
Whipstitch to C.
Whipstitch to one D.

B – Holder Front
(cut 1) 13 x 32 holes

Whipstitch to one D.
Cut Out
Whipstitch to E.
Whipstitch to one D.

COLOR KEY: Bunny Hop

Embroidery floss			AMOUNT
■ Red			1 yd.

Worsted-weight	Nylon Plus™	Need-loft®	YARN AMOUNT
☐ White	#01	#41	38 yds.
▨ Lavender	#22	#45	18 yds.
▨ Dk. Green	#31	#27	10 yds.
▨ Pink	#11	#07	10 yds.
■ Black	#02	#00	4 yds.
▨ Sea Green	#37	#53	2 yds.
▨ Yellow	#26	#57	2 yds.
▨ Watermelon	#54	#55	1 yd.

STITCH KEY:
— Backstitch/Straight Stitch
☐ Unworked Area/Holder Front Attachment

Holder Assembly Diagram

Step 1:
With dk. green, Whipstitch bottom edges of B-D pieces to right side of E.

Step 2:
With pink, Whipstitch B-D pieces together; Overcast unfinished edges of fence.

Biblical Accents

Designed by Trudy Bath Smith

SIZE: Each Bookmark is 2¼" x 7¾"; Bible Box is ⅞" x 1¾" x 2½", not including place markers; each optional Pin is about ½" x 1".

MATERIALS: One sheet of 10-count plastic canvas; Two sheets each of black and white 14-count plastic canvas; Craft glue or glue gun; Six-strand embroidery floss (for amounts see Color Key on page 93); Fine metallic braid (for amount see Color Key); ⅛" metallic ribbon (for amounts see Color Key).

NOTE: Graphs on pages 92 & 93.
For each optional Pin, cut and stitch additional motif according to Bookmark C graph of choice; glue pinback to wrong side.

BOOKMARKS

CUTTING INSTRUCTIONS:

A: For backs, cut seven from black 14-count according to graph.

B: For fronts, cut seven from white 14-count according to graph.

C: For motifs, cut one each from 10-count according to graphs.

STITCHING INSTRUCTIONS:

1: Using colors and stitches indicated, work C pieces according to graphs; with turquoise for Matthew fish, with colors indicated on Genesis rainbow C graph and with matching colors, Overcast unfinished edges. Using purple ribbon and Backstitch, embroider detail on Joshua crown C as indicated.

2: Centering one Bible reference on each front, using braid and three strands black or desired color floss, work B pieces according to stitch pattern guides.

3: For each Bookmark, centering one B on one A, using three strands black or desired color floss and Running Stitch, work outlines through both thicknesses according to B graph; for front with optional cutout, work Running Stitch around cutout also.

4: Glue corresponding C piece to each Bookmark as shown in photo or as desired.✧

BIBLE BOX

CUTTING INSTRUCTIONS:

NOTE: Use black 14-count for A and white 14-count canvas for remaining pieces.

A: For cover, cut one 34 x 56 holes.

B: For front, cut one according to graph.

C: For sides, cut two according to graph.

D: For drawer front, cut one according to graph.

E: For drawer sides, cut two from white 14-count 5 x 18 holes (no graph).

F: For drawer back, cut one from white 14-count 5 x 22 holes (no graph).

G: For drawer bottom, cut one from white 14-count 18 x 22 holes (no graph).

STITCHING INSTRUCTIONS:

NOTES: B-G pieces are unworked.
Use doubled strand of braid throughout.

1: Using braid and stitches indicated, work A according to graph.

NOTE: For place markers, cut one 1½" length each of pink, purple and turquoise ribbon.

2: Whipstitch A-C pieces and place markers together as indicated and according to Bible Box Assembly Diagram on page 93. For drawer, with three strands white floss, Whipstitch D-G pieces together according to Drawer Assembly Diagram. Place drawer in Bible Box as shown in photo.✧

Drawer Assembly Diagram

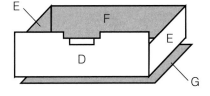

Biblical Accents

PHOTO ON PAGE 90

A – Bible Box Cover
(cut 1 from black) 34 x 56 holes

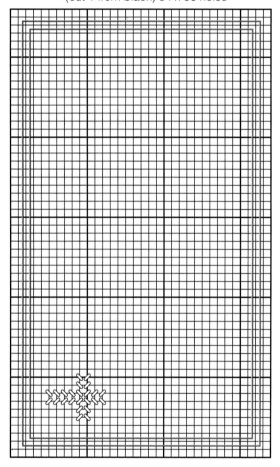

B – Bible Box Front
(cut 1 from white) 10 x 30 holes

Cut Out

C – Bible Box Side
(cut 2 from white) 10 x 22 holes

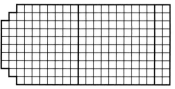

D – Bible Box Drawer Front
(cut 1 from white)
7 x 22 holes

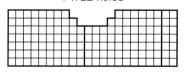

A – Bookmark Back
(cut 7 from black)
30 x 108 holes

B – Bookmark Front
(cut 7 from white)
22 x 100 holes

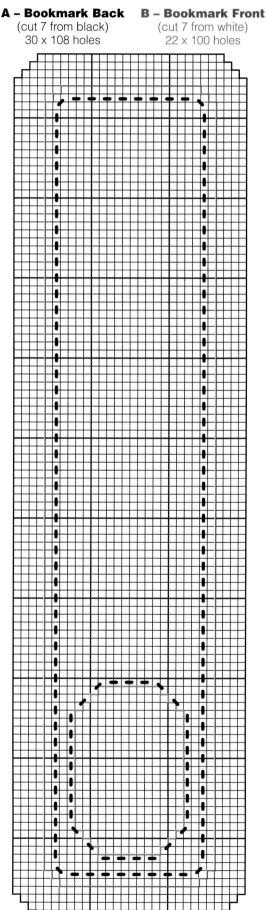

COLOR KEY: Biblical Accents

Embroidery floss

		AMOUNT
☐	Blue	8 yds.
■	Black	6 yds.
☐	White	1 yd.

Kreinik #8 metallic braid	**Metallic braid**	AMOUNT
▨ #210 Gold Dust	Gold	7½ yds.

Kreinik metallic ribbon	**Metallic ribbon**	AMOUNT
▨ #002 Gold	Gold	2 yds.
☐ #012 Purple	Purple	½ yd.
▨ #028 Citron	Yellow	2 yds.
▨ #033 Royal	Dk. Blue	2 yds.
▨ #092 Star Pink	Pink	1½ yds.
▨ #094 Star Blue	Turquoise	1½ yds.

STITCH KEY:

- — Backstitch/Straight Stitch
- ☐ Cutout for optional front only.
- ☐ Front/Side Assembly Attachment

Bible Box Assembly Diagram
(underside view)

Step 1: With three strands white floss, Whipstitch B and C pieces together.

Place Markers

Step 2: Fold A over B/C assembly; with braid, Whipstitch together, catching ends of place markers as you work.

Galatians Stitch Pattern Guide

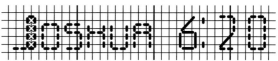

Genesis Stitch Pattern Guide

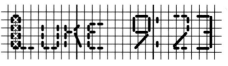

Isaiah Stitch Pattern Guide

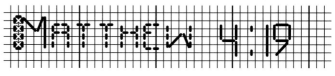

**C – Bookmark
Galatians Heart**
(cut 1 from clear)
7 x 7 holes

**C – Bookmark
Genesis Rainbow**
(cut 1 from clear)
5 x 9 holes

Overcast with pink between pink arrows.

Overcast with purple between purple arrows.

**C – Bookmark
Isaiah Trumpet**
(cut 1 from clear)
9 x 15 holes

Cut out gray area.

**C – Bookmark
Malachi Sun**
(cut 1 from clear)
13 x 13 holes

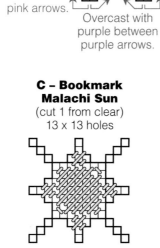

Joshua Stitch Pattern Guide

**C – Bookmark
Joshua Crown**
(cut 1 from clear)
5 x 11 holes

Luke Stitch Pattern Guide

**C – Bookmark
Matthew Fish**
(cut 1 from clear)
9 x 9 holes

Cut out gray area carefully.

**C – Bookmark
Luke Cross**
(cut 1 from clear)
8 x 11 holes

Matthew Stitch Pattern Guide

Malachi Stitch Pattern Guide

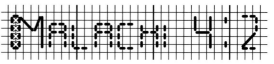

Cottontail Cuties

Designed by
Rebecca Keirn

SIZE: Notepad Holder is 1½" x 6½" x 7½" tall and holds a 3" x 5" notepad; Tulip Fridgie is 2" x 3".

MATERIALS: One sheet of 7-count plastic canvas; Four blue and one green 4-mm wiggle eyes; One white ½" pom-pom; Magnetic strips; Craft glue or glue gun; Six-strand embroidery floss (for amount see Color Key); Pearlized metallic cord (for amount see Color Key); Metallic cord (for amounts see Color Key); Worsted-weight or plastic canvas yarn (for amounts see Color Key).

CUTTING INSTRUCTIONS:

A: For Notepad Holder back, cut one according to graph.

B: For pad compartment front, cut one according to graph.

C: For pad compartment sides, cut two 4 x 12 holes (no graph).

D: For pad/pen compartment bottom, cut one 8 x 23 holes.

E: For pen compartment front, cut one according to graph.

F: For bow, cut one according to graph.

G: For Tulip, cut one according to graph.

STITCHING INSTRUCTIONS:

1: Using yarn and cord in colors and stitches indicated, work A, B and D-G (leave indicated area of D unworked) pieces according to graphs; fill in uncoded areas of A (leave indicated area unworked) and B pieces using white yarn and Continental Stitch. Using moss and Continental Stitch, work C pieces. With yellow yarn for bow, pumpkin yarn for duck's beak as shown in photo and with matching colors, Overcast edges of A, F and G pieces; Overcast edges of B and E pieces as indicated on graphs.

2: Using six strands floss, Backstitch and Straight Stitch, embroider noses and mouths on bunnies as indicated on A and B graphs.

Using yarn in colors indicated, Backstitch and Straight Stitch, embroider outlines and flower and leaf detail as indicated on A, B, E and G graphs.

3: With white for bunny body and with moss, Whipstitch B-E pieces together as indicated and according to Pad/Pen Compartment Assembly Diagram. With moss, Whipstitch sides and bottom of compartment assembly to indicated area on right side of A; Overcast unfinished edges of compartment sides.

4: Glue bow to Notepad Holder, two blue wiggle eyes to each bunny and green wiggle eye to duck as shown. Glue magnetic strips to back of Notepad Holder and Tulip.✧

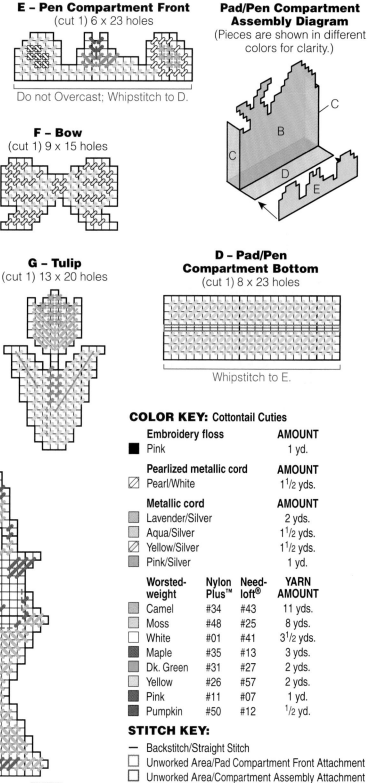

E – Pen Compartment Front
(cut 1) 6 x 23 holes

Do not Overcast; Whipstitch to D.

Pad/Pen Compartment Assembly Diagram
(Pieces are shown in different colors for clarity.)

F – Bow
(cut 1) 9 x 15 holes

G – Tulip
(cut 1) 13 x 20 holes

D – Pad/Pen Compartment Bottom
(cut 1) 8 x 23 holes

Whipstitch to E.

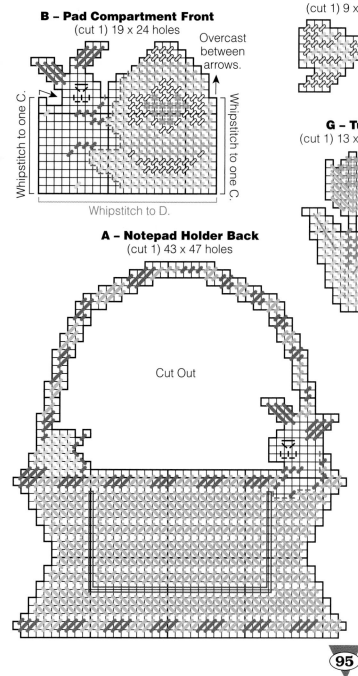

B – Pad Compartment Front
(cut 1) 19 x 24 holes

Overcast between arrows.

Whipstitch to one C.

Whipstitch to one C.

Whipstitch to D.

A – Notepad Holder Back
(cut 1) 43 x 47 holes

Cut Out

COLOR KEY: Cottontail Cuties

Embroidery floss		AMOUNT
■ Pink		1 yd.

Pearlized metallic cord		AMOUNT
▨ Pearl/White		1¹/₂ yds.

Metallic cord		AMOUNT
▨ Lavender/Silver		2 yds.
▨ Aqua/Silver		1¹/₂ yds.
▨ Yellow/Silver		1¹/₂ yds.
▨ Pink/Silver		1 yd.

Worsted-weight	Nylon Plus™	Need-loft®	YARN AMOUNT
▨ Camel	#34	#43	11 yds.
▨ Moss	#48	#25	8 yds.
▢ White	#01	#41	3¹/₂ yds.
▨ Maple	#35	#13	3 yds.
▨ Dk. Green	#31	#27	2 yds.
▨ Yellow	#26	#57	2 yds.
▨ Pink	#11	#07	1 yd.
▨ Pumpkin	#50	#12	¹/₂ yd.

STITCH KEY:

— Backstitch/Straight Stitch
▢ Unworked Area/Pad Compartment Front Attachment
▢ Unworked Area/Compartment Assembly Attachment

God's Promise

Designed by Fran Rohus

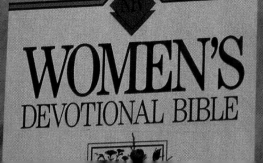

SIZE: 8⅝" x 10⅜".

MATERIALS: One sheet of 7-count plastic canvas; Worsted-weight or plastic canvas yarn (for amounts see Color Key).

CUTTING INSTRUCTIONS:

A: For Wall Plaque, cut one according to graph.

STITCHING INSTRUCTIONS:

1: Using colors and stitches indicated, work A according to graph; fill in uncoded areas using white and Continental Stitch. With purple, Overcast edges.

NOTE: Separate remaining purple and turquoise into 2-ply or nylon plastic canvas yarn into 1-ply strands.

2: Using 2-ply (or 1-ply) colors indicated, Backstitch, Straight Stitch and French Knot, embroider letter detail as indicated.

3: Display as shown in photo or as desired.✧

COLOR KEY: God's Promise

	Worsted-weight	Nylon Plus™	Need-loft®	YARN AMOUNT
☐	White	#01	#41	34 yds.
▨	Purple	#21	#46	14 yds.
▨	Watermelon	#54	#55	6 yds.
▨	Turquoise	#03	#54	4 yds.
▨	Yellow	#26	#57	2 yds.
■	Dk. Brown	#36	#15	1 yd.

STITCH KEY:

- — Backstitch/Straight Stitch
- • French Knot

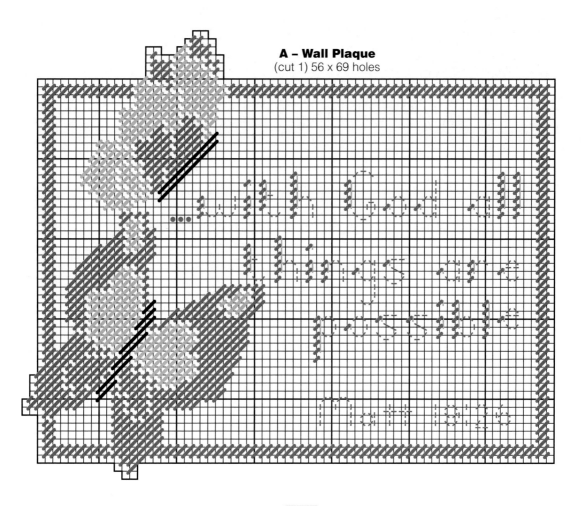

A – Wall Plaque
(cut 1) 56 x 69 holes

Mr. & Mrs. Rabbit

Designed by Suzanne Varnell

SIZE: 11" x 14" x 13½" tall.

MATERIALS: One 13½" x 22½" sheet and ½ standard-size sheet of 7-count plastic canvas; ½ sheet of 10-count plastic canvas; One 11" x 14" decorative wood plaque; 12 wooden ⅝" x ⅞" eggs; Four wooden ⅝" x 1½" carrots; Two 11¼" wooden ¼" dowels; Drill and ⁷⁄₆₄" and ¼" round wood drill bits; Desired colors of paint; Spanish moss or excelsior; 1 yd. of ⅛" jute; Craft glue or glue gun; Six-strand embroidery floss (for amounts see Color Key on page 101); Worsted-weight or plastic canvas yarn (for amounts see Color Key).

CUTTING INSTRUCTIONS:

NOTE: Graphs on pages 100 & 101.
Use 10-count for E-G and 7-count canvas for remaining pieces.

A: For bunnies, cut one according to graph.
B: For basket short and long sides, cut four 9 x 9 holes for short sides and four 9 x 15 holes for long sides (no graphs).
C: For basket bottoms, cut two 9 x 15 holes (no graph).
D: For basket handles, cut two 3 x 39 holes (no graph).
E: For bunny noses, cut two according to graph.
F: For bunny buttons, cut four according to graph.
G: For sign, cut one according to graph.

STITCHING INSTRUCTIONS:

NOTES: Paint plaque for base, dowels, eggs and carrots as desired (see photo); let dry.

Separate cinnamon into 2-ply or nylon plastic canvas yarn into 1-ply strands; use 2-ply (or 1-ply) cinnamon throughout.

C pieces are unworked.

1: Using yarn and six strands floss in colors and stitches indicated, work A and E pieces according to graphs; fill in uncoded areas of A using white yarn and Continental Stitch. Using cinnamon and Continental Stitch, work G.

Using watermelon and Slanted Gobelin Stitch over narrow width, work two long B, two short B and one D piece; substituting lt. blue for watermelon, repeat with remaining B and D pieces. With six strands black floss for buttons and with matching colors, Overcast edges of A and D-G (omit cutout edges on G) pieces.

2: Using six strands black floss, Backstitch, Straight Stitch and French Knot, embroider facial features and outlines as indicated on A graph. Using three strands white floss and Backstitch, embroider letters as indicated on G graph.

3: For each basket, with matching color, Whipstitch one C and two of each matching color B pieces together; Overcast unfinished edges. Glue matching color handle to basket long sides as shown in photo.

NOTES: Cut jute into four 9" lengths.

Using ⁷⁄₁₆" bit, drill a hole from front to back in center of each carrot top through entire thickness.

4: To attach carrots to each bunny, thread each end of one 9" strand of jute from back to front through one ♦ hole on one bunny as indicated, then through hole of one carrot (see photo); pull ends to even, then tie ends into a bow and trim. To attach sign to each bunny, thread each end of one 9" strand from back to front through one ♦ hole (same holes as used for carrot attachment) on one bunny, then through one cutout on one end of sign as indicated (see photo); tie ends into a bow and trim.

5: To determine locations for support dowels, stand bunnies on base as desired or as shown. Working behind bunnies, mark on base where center bottom of each bunny is located; set bunnies aside. With ¼" bit, drill a hole about ¼" deep in base at each mark.

6: Glue one dowel inside each hole in base, back of bunnies to dowels and bottom of bunnies to base; glue one nose and two buttons to each bunny and Spanish moss or excelsior to base. Glue baskets and eggs together and to base as desired or as shown. ✧

Mr. & Mrs. Rabbit

PHOTO ON PAGE 98

A – Bunnies
(cut 1 from 7-count) 84 x 94 holes

Cut Out

G – Sign
(cut 1 from 10-count) 10 x 73 holes

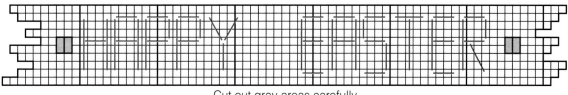

Cut out gray areas carefully.

E – Bunny Nose
(cut 2 from 10-count)
4 x 5 holes

F – Bunny Button
(cut 4 from 10-count)
3 x 3 holes

COLOR KEY: Mr. & Mrs. Rabbit

Embroidery floss			AMOUNT
■ Black			8 yds.
■ Dk. Pink			2 yds.
■ White			2 yds.

Worsted-weight	Nylon Plus™	Need-loft®	YARN AMOUNT
☐ White	#01	#41	45 yds.
▨ Peach	#46	#47	20 yds.
▨ Turquoise	#03	#54	20 yds.
☐ Lt. Blue	#05	#36	8 yds.
☐ Watermelon	#54	#55	8 yds.
☐ Cinnamon	#44	#14	5 yds.
▨ Pink	#11	#07	4 yds.
▨ Flesh	#14	#56	1 yd.
▨ Lt. Green	#28	#26	1 yd.

STITCH KEY:

— Backstitch/Straight Stitch
● French Knot

Carrot Shoppe

Designed by Gina Woods

Take a springtime stroll through this precious Easter village.

SIZE: 4¾" x 9¼" x 6⅛" tall.

MATERIALS: One sheet of clear stiff, ½ sheet of neon lime and scraps of white and pink 7-count plastic canvas; Scrap of clear 10-count plastic canvas; Two 1½"-tall flocked bunnies; 12 transparent emerald 4-mm round faceted beads; Three emerald 10- x 12-mm heart-shaped pony beads; Scraps of rose, green and orange felt; Scraps of sculpted lace with scalloped motifs; 6" moss chenille stem; Craft glue or glue gun; Six-strand embroidery floss (for amounts see Color Key on page 105); Worsted-weight or plastic canvas yarn (for amounts see Color Key).

CUTTING INSTRUCTIONS:

NOTE: Graphs on pages 104 & 105. Use 10-count for I and 7-count canvas for remaining pieces.

A: For back, cut one from stiff according to graph.

B: For bottom, cut one from stiff according to graph.

C: For pink building small and large roofs, cut one each from stiff according to graphs.

D: For pink building window box, cut one from stiff 2 x 9 holes.

E: For pink building small and large window frames, cut number needed from pink according to graphs.

F: For purple building roof, cut one from stiff 4 x 24 holes.

G: For purple building shutters #1 and #2, cut one each from stiff 3 x 6 holes.

H: For purple building window frame, cut one from lime according to graph.

I: For purple building sign, cut one from 10-count 3 x 20 holes.

J: For yellow building roof, cut one from stiff according to graph.

K: For yellow building door, cut one from stiff 4 x 9 holes.

L: For yellow building balcony front and sides, cut number needed from white according to graphs.

M: For yellow building balcony floor, cut one from stiff 5 x 14 holes (no graph).

N: For yellow building window awning, cut one from stiff 6 x 9 holes.

O: For fence front, cut one from lime according to graph.

P: For fence sides, cut two from lime according to graph.

Q: For carrot motif, cut one from orange felt according to Carrot Motif Pattern.

R: For carrot top motif, cut one from green felt according to Carrot Top Motif Pattern.

S: For heart, cut one from rose felt according to Heart Pattern.

T: For purple building roof motif, cut one from green felt according to Purple Building Roof Motif Pattern.

STITCHING INSTRUCTIONS:

1: Using yarn in colors and stitches indicated, work A-D, J, K and N pieces according to graphs; using white and Continental Stitch, work F, G and M pieces. With matching colors, Overcast edges of C, F and J pieces, steps on B as indicated on graph and D as indicated. Using 12 strands white floss and Continental Stitch, work I; Overcast edges.

NOTES: Separate orange, dk. green and 1 yd. of fern into 2-ply or nylon plastic canvas yarn into 1-ply strands. Cut six 3" lengths of fern.

2: Using 2-ply (or 1-ply) yarn in colors indicated and Straight Stitch, embroider carrots as indicated on F and G graphs. Using fern and Lazy Daisy Stitch, embroider grass as indicated on A graph. For window box carrot garden (see photo), attach one 3" strand of fern with Lark's Head Knot in each ♦ hole on D as indicated; trim and fray ends close to knots.

3: Holding large E to matching cutout area on wrong side of A, with white, Whipstitch outer edges together; substituting rose for white, repeat as above to attach small E pieces at matching cutout areas on A.

4: Holding H to wrong side and G pieces to right side of cutout area on A as indicated, with white, Whipstitch together through all thicknesses; Overcast unfinished edges of shutters. With gold, Whipstitch K to cutout area on right side of A as indicated; Overcast unfinished edges of door frame and door.

5: Using 12 strands dk. blue floss and Straight Stitch, embroider sign outline on purple building as indicated on A graph (see photo). Using six strands floss in colors indicated, Backstitch, Straight Stitch and French Knot, embroider roof and door detail, window and door outlines and letters as indicated on A, C, I and K graphs.

Carrot Shoppe

CONTINUED FROM PAGE 103

6: With gold, Whipstitch N to right side of A as indicated; Overcast edges of window awning. For balcony, with white and omitting front corners of rails, Whipstitch L and M pieces together; Whipstitch balcony sides and floor to indicated area on right side of A.

7: Omitting front corners of fence, with fern, Whipstitch A, B, O and P pieces together as indi-cated; with white for sides as shown in photo and with matching colors, Overcast unfinished edges of A, catching ends of each fence side to back as you work to secure.

8: Glue lace and felt motifs, bunnies and worked pieces together and to Carrot Shoppe as shown. Bend chenille around gate front and glue to secure, trimming away excess as needed to fit (see photo). Glue round beads onto short spikes around fence, one heart bead onto corner pair of spikes at each fence side and remaining heart bead to gate as shown. ✧

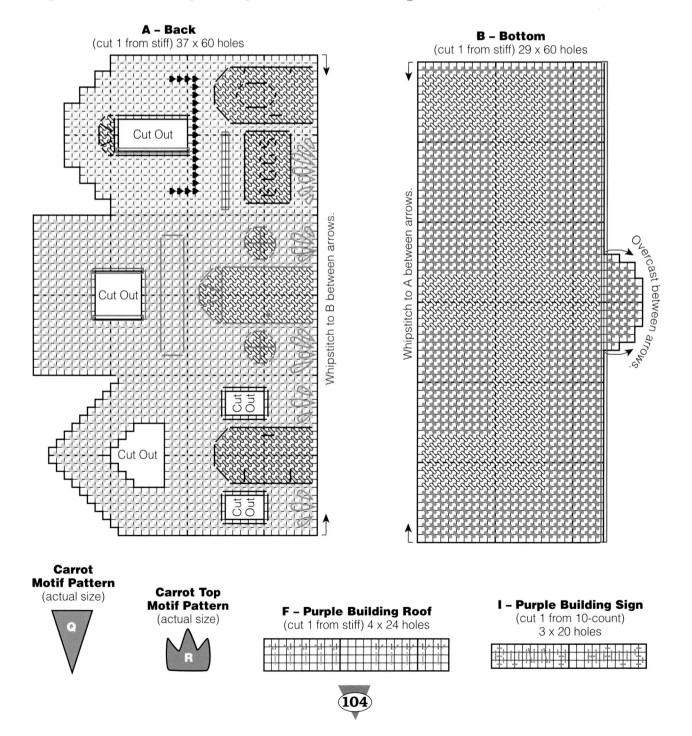

A – Back
(cut 1 from stiff) 37 x 60 holes

Whipstitch to B between arrows.

B – Bottom
(cut 1 from stiff) 29 x 60 holes

Whipstitch to A between arrows.

Overcast between arrows.

Carrot Motif Pattern
(actual size)

Carrot Top Motif Pattern
(actual size)

F – Purple Building Roof
(cut 1 from stiff) 4 x 24 holes

I – Purple Building Sign
(cut 1 from 10-count)
3 x 20 holes

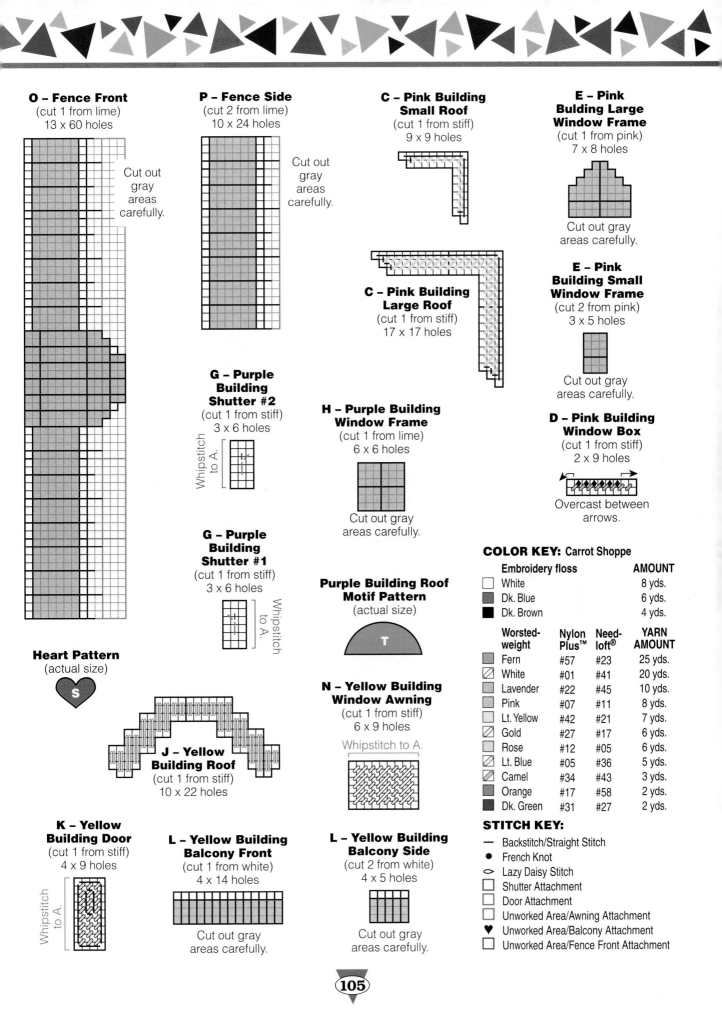

O – Fence Front
(cut 1 from lime)
13 x 60 holes

Cut out gray areas carefully.

P – Fence Side
(cut 2 from lime)
10 x 24 holes

Cut out gray areas carefully.

C – Pink Building Small Roof
(cut 1 from stiff)
9 x 9 holes

C – Pink Building Large Roof
(cut 1 from stiff)
17 x 17 holes

E – Pink Bulding Large Window Frame
(cut 1 from pink)
7 x 8 holes

Cut out gray areas carefully.

E – Pink Building Small Window Frame
(cut 2 from pink)
3 x 5 holes

Cut out gray areas carefully.

D – Pink Building Window Box
(cut 1 from stiff)
2 x 9 holes

Overcast between arrows.

G – Purple Building Shutter #2
(cut 1 from stiff)
3 x 6 holes

Whipstitch to A.

G – Purple Building Shutter #1
(cut 1 from stiff)
3 x 6 holes

Whipstitch to A.

H – Purple Building Window Frame
(cut 1 from lime)
6 x 6 holes

Cut out gray areas carefully.

Purple Building Roof Motif Pattern
(actual size)

T

Heart Pattern
(actual size)

S

J – Yellow Building Roof
(cut 1 from stiff)
10 x 22 holes

N – Yellow Building Window Awning
(cut 1 from stiff)
6 x 9 holes

Whipstitch to A.

K – Yellow Building Door
(cut 1 from stiff)
4 x 9 holes

Whipstitch to A.

L – Yellow Building Balcony Front
(cut 1 from white)
4 x 14 holes

Cut out gray areas carefully.

L – Yellow Building Balcony Side
(cut 2 from white)
4 x 5 holes

Cut out gray areas carefully.

COLOR KEY: Carrot Shoppe

Embroidery floss			AMOUNT
White			8 yds.
Dk. Blue			6 yds.
Dk. Brown			4 yds.

Worsted-weight	Nylon Plus™	Need-loft®	YARN AMOUNT
Fern	#57	#23	25 yds.
White	#01	#41	20 yds.
Lavender	#22	#45	10 yds.
Pink	#07	#11	8 yds.
Lt. Yellow	#42	#21	7 yds.
Gold	#27	#17	6 yds.
Rose	#12	#05	6 yds.
Lt. Blue	#05	#36	5 yds.
Camel	#34	#43	3 yds.
Orange	#17	#58	2 yds.
Dk. Green	#31	#27	2 yds.

STITCH KEY:
— Backstitch/Straight Stitch
• French Knot
⌒ Lazy Daisy Stitch
☐ Shutter Attachment
☐ Door Attachment
☐ Unworked Area/Awning Attachment
♥ Unworked Area/Balcony Attachment
☐ Unworked Area/Fence Front Attachment

Fabric photographed with permission of Santee Print Works, New York, New York

Goblin Gathering

On Halloween
night, the screech owl
screams of coming doom and
a witch flies wild across the moon.
Bubble, bubble, toil and trouble…Treat
the spooks at your house to a cauldron full of
fun, and conjure up a haunted house full
of surprises when you welcome
your friends with a
fearful collection
of clever
decorations.

Jack-o-Lantern Box

Designed by Nancy Marshall

SIZE: 3⅛" x 4⅝" x 6" tall.

MATERIALS: One sheet of 7-count plastic canvas; Worsted-weight or plastic canvas yarn (for amounts see Color Key).

CUTTING INSTRUCTIONS:

A: For front and back, cut two (one for front and one for back) according to graph.

B: For sides, cut two 11 x 27 holes (no graph).

C: For bottom, cut one 11 x 17 holes (no graph).

D: For hat brim, cut one according to graph.

E: For hat crown, cut two according to graph.

F: For lid lip long sides, cut two 4 x 15 holes (no graph).

G: For lid lip short sides, cut two 4 x 10 holes (no graph).

STITCHING INSTRUCTIONS:

NOTE: C, F and G pieces are unworked.

1: Using colors and stitches indicated, work one A for front, B, D (leave indicated areas unworked) and E pieces according to graphs and stitch pattern guide; omitting facial features, work remaining A for back according to background pattern established on front.

2: For box, with orange, Whipstitch A-C pieces together as indicated on A graph; Overcast unfinished edges. For hat, with black, Whipstitch D-G pieces together as indicated and according to Hat Assembly Diagram; Overcast unfinished edges of brim.✧

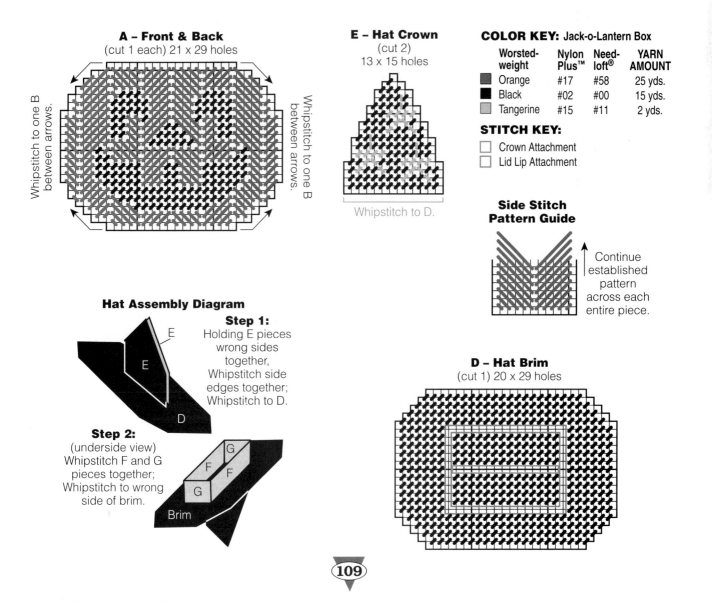

A – Front & Back
(cut 1 each) 21 x 29 holes

Whipstitch to one B between arrows.

Whipstitch to one B between arrows.

E – Hat Crown
(cut 2)
13 x 15 holes

Whipstitch to D.

COLOR KEY: Jack-o-Lantern Box

	Worsted-weight	Nylon Plus™	Need-loft®	YARN AMOUNT
▨	Orange	#17	#58	25 yds.
■	Black	#02	#00	15 yds.
▨	Tangerine	#15	#11	2 yds.

STITCH KEY:
☐ Crown Attachment
☐ Lid Lip Attachment

Side Stitch Pattern Guide

Continue established pattern across each entire piece.

Hat Assembly Diagram

Step 1:
Holding E pieces wrong sides together, Whipstitch side edges together; Whipstitch to D.

E
E
D

Step 2:
(underside view) Whipstitch F and G pieces together; Whipstitch to wrong side of brim.

G G
F F
G
Brim

D – Hat Brim
(cut 1) 20 x 29 holes

Halloween Greeting

Designed by Patricia Klesh

SIZE: 9¼" x 20⅝".

MATERIALS: Two sheets of 7-count plastic canvas; One off-white 1" plastic ring; Craft glue or glue gun; Six-strand embroidery floss (for amount see Color Key); Worsted-weight or plastic canvas yarn (for amounts see Color Key).

CUTTING INSTRUCTIONS:

A: For ghost, cut one according to graph.

B: For ghost arm, cut one according to graph.

C: For pumpkins #1 and #2, cut one each according to graphs.

D: For pumpkin stems, cut two according to graph.

E: For vine, cut one according to graph.

F: For leaves, cut three according to graph.

STITCHING INSTRUCTIONS:

1: Using colors and stitches indicated, work A-F (one D on opposite side of canvas) pieces according to graphs. With white, Whipstitch A and B pieces together as indicated on graphs. With matching colors, Overcast unfinished edges of A-F pieces.

2: Using six strands floss and Backstitch, embroider eye outlines as indicated on C graphs.

3: With white, Whipstitch plastic ring to top of ghost; glue pieces together as shown in photo.✧

C – Pumpkin #1
(cut 1) 23 x 26 holes

B – Ghost Arm
(cut 1)
14 x 14 holes

Whipstitch to A.

A – Ghost
(cut 1)
51 x 56 holes

Whipstitch to B.

C – Pumpkin #2
(cut 1) 23 x 26 holes

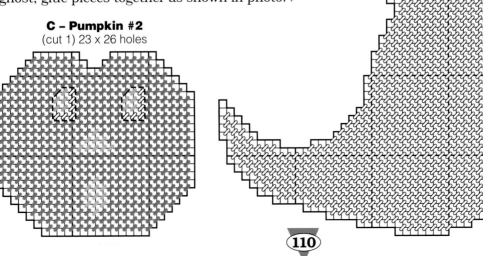

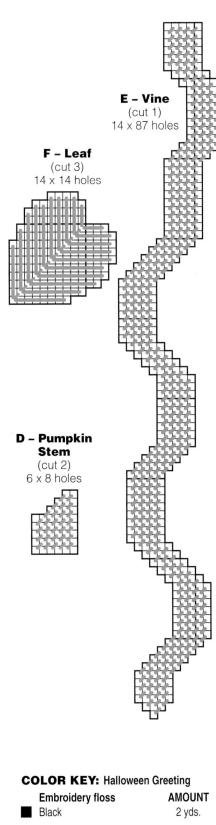

E – Vine
(cut 1)
14 x 87 holes

F – Leaf
(cut 3)
14 x 14 holes

D – Pumpkin Stem
(cut 2)
6 x 8 holes

COLOR KEY: Halloween Greeting

	Embroidery floss			AMOUNT
■	Black			2 yds.

	Worsted-weight	Nylon Plus™	Need-loft®	YARN AMOUNT
▨	White	#01	#41	24 yds.
	Dk. Green	#31	#27	19 yds.
	Orange	#17	#58	18 yds.
	Black	#02	#00	4 yds.
	Camel	#34	#43	3 yds.

STITCH KEY:
— Backstitch/Straight Stitch

Kitty Candy Dish

Designed by Judy L. Nelson

SIZE: 4" x 11⅛" x 5¾" tall above top of table.

MATERIALS: Four sheets of 7-count plastic canvas; 1½ yds. orange ⅛" satin ribbon; Six black plastic animal whiskers; Craft glue or glue gun; Six-strand embroidery floss (for amount see Color Key); Worsted-weight or plastic canvas yarn (for amounts see Color Key).

CUTTING INSTRUCTIONS:

A: For body, cut two according to graph.

B: For head, cut two according to graph.

C: For box back, cut two 18 x 54 holes (no graph).

D: For box ends, cut four 18 x 23 holes (no graph).

E: For bottom, cut two 23 x 54 holes (no graph).

F: For sign, cut one 18 x 29 holes.

STITCHING INSTRUCTIONS:

NOTE: E pieces are unworked.

1: Holding two matching pieces together and working through both thicknesses as one, using colors and stitches indicated, work A (leave uncoded areas unworked) and B pieces according to graphs; using black and Continental Stitch, work C and D pieces. Using white and Continental Stitch, work F.

2: With black, Whipstitch body, box ends and box back together as indicated on graph and according to Cat Assembly Diagram. Whipstitch unfinished top edges of box together and of body together; Whipstitch unfinished edges of head together. With orange, Overcast edges of F.

3: Using six strands floss and yarn in colors indicated, Backstitch and Straight

112

Stitch, embroider detail on body and head and letters on sign as indicated.

NOTE: Cut ribbon in half.

4: Holding ribbons together and leaving tails at least 9" long, thread ribbons from front to back through sign at one ◆ hole as indicated, then through several stitches on wrong side of extended paw (see photo); thread from back to front through remaining ◆ hole. At each corner, tie ribbon ends into a small bow; trim ends.

5: Glue three whiskers to each side of nose and head to body as shown.✧

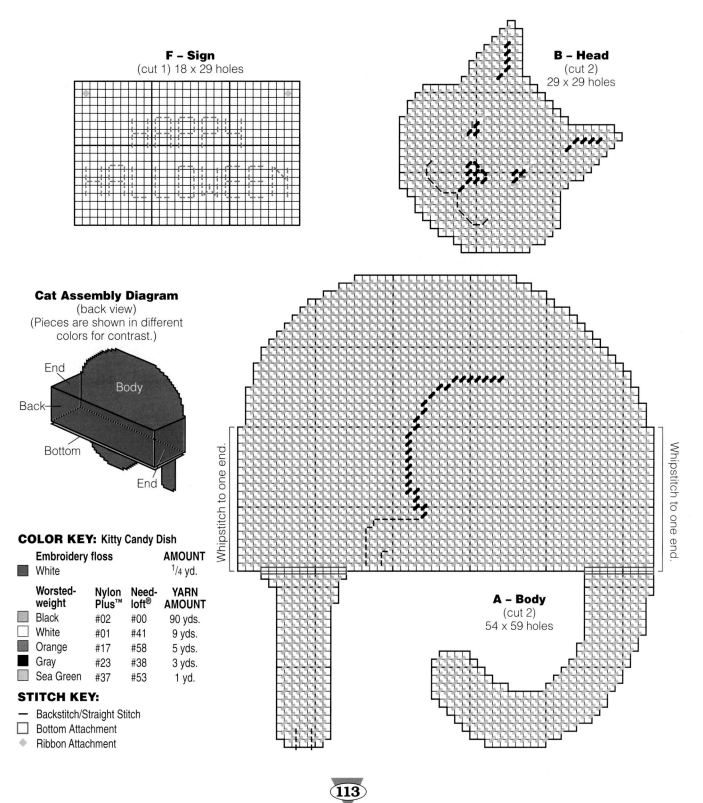

F – Sign
(cut 1) 18 x 29 holes

HAPPY
HALLOWEEN

B – Head
(cut 2)
29 x 29 holes

Cat Assembly Diagram
(back view)
(Pieces are shown in different colors for contrast.)

End
Body
Back
Bottom
End

Whipstitch to one end.

Whipstitch to one end.

A – Body
(cut 2)
54 x 59 holes

COLOR KEY: Kitty Candy Dish

Embroidery floss			AMOUNT
White			1/4 yd.

Worsted-weight	Nylon Plus™	Need-loft®	YARN AMOUNT
Black	#02	#00	90 yds.
White	#01	#41	9 yds.
Orange	#17	#58	5 yds.
Gray	#23	#38	3 yds.
Sea Green	#37	#53	1 yd.

STITCH KEY:
— Backstitch/Straight Stitch
☐ Bottom Attachment
◆ Ribbon Attachment

113

Trick-or-Treat Tote

Designed by Robin Petrina

SIZE: 3⅞" x 10¾" x 8⅜" tall, not including handles.

MATERIALS: Three sheets of orange 7-count platic canvas; Worsted-weight or plastic canvas yarn (for amounts see Color Key).

CUTTING INSTRUCTIONS:

A: For front and back, cut two (one for front and one for back) 55 x 70 holes (no back graph).
B: For sides, cut two 25 x 55 holes (no graph).
C: For bottom, cut one 25 x 70 holes (no graph).
D: For handles, cut two 6 x 90 holes (no graph).

STITCHING INSTRUCTIONS:

NOTE: Back A and B-D pieces are unworked.

1: Omitting handle attachment areas, using colors and stitches indicated, work one A for front according to graph. With orange, Overcast D pieces. Using black and Backstitch, embroider ghost eye and nose detail and letter outlines as indicated on graph.

NOTE: Separate ½ yd. of orange into 2-ply or nylon plastic canvas yarn into 1-ply strands.

2: Using 2-ply (or 1-ply) orange and French Knot, embroider bat eyes as indicated.

3: To join one handle to front, holding ends of one D to wrong side of front at top edge as indicated, using orange and stitches indicated, work through both thicknesses as one according to graph. Repeat with remaining handle and back.

4: With orange, Whipstitch A-C pieces together; Overcast unfinished edges.✧

STITCH KEY:
- — Backstitch/Straight Stitch
- • French Knot
- ☐ Handle Attachment

COLOR KEY: Trick-or-Treat Tote

	Worsted-weight	Nylon Plus™	Need-loft®	YARN AMOUNT
▨	Orange	#17	#58	15 yds.
▨	White	#01	#41	12 yds.
■	Black	#02	#00	5 yds.

A – Front (cut 1) 55 x 70 holes

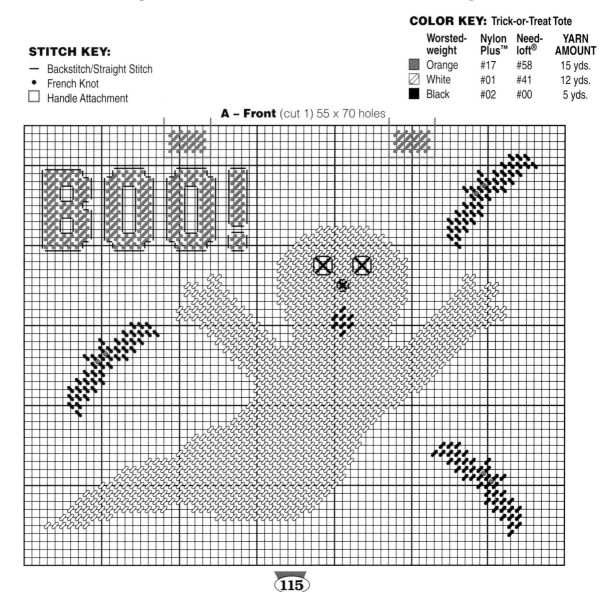

Goblins Galore

Designed by Stephen E. Reedy

*Whip up a batch of
clever coasters for
your spooky party table.*

Instructions on next page

Goblins Galore

PHOTO ON PAGES 116 & 117

SIZE: Each Coaster is 3⅞" square.

MATERIALS: Three sheets of 7-count plastic canvas; Six-strand embroidery floss (for amount see Color Key); Worsted-weight or plastic canvas yarn (for amounts see Color Key).

CUTTING INSTRUCTIONS:

A: For Coasters, cut eight 25 x 25 holes.
B: For Coaster backings, cut eight from clear 25 x 25 holes (no graph).

STITCHING INSTRUCTIONS:

NOTE: B pieces are unworked.

1: Using colors and stitches indicated, work one A (Use a double strand of orange for witch's hair as needed.) according to each graph.

2: Using colors indicated, French Knot and Straight Stitch, embroider Frankenstein's eyes, Dracula's mouth detail, witch's broom and skull's nose as indicated on graphs.

NOTE: Separate floss into 3-ply strands; separate 1 yd. of black and remaining red into 2-ply or nylon plastic canvas yarn into 1-ply strands.

3: Using three strands floss for Jack-o-Lantern detail and 2-ply (or 1-ply) colors indicated, French Knot, Backstitch and Straight Stitch, embroider detail on Pumpkin, Scarecrow and Graveyard and remaining detail on Frankenstein, Dracula and Witch as indicated.

4: For each Coaster, holding one B to wrong side of one A, with matching background color, Whipstitch together. ✧

COLOR KEY: Goblins Galore

Embroidery floss			AMOUNT
▨ Black			2 yds.

Worsted-weight	Nylon Plus™	Need-loft®	YARN AMOUNT
■ Black	#02	#00	34 yds.
▢ Yellow	#26	#57	32 yds.
▨ White	#01	#41	12 yds.
▨ Orange	#17	#58	6 yds.
▨ Bt. Green		#61	5 yds.
▨ Cinnamon	#44	#14	3 yds.
▢ Camel	#34	#43	2 yds.
■ Purple	#21	#46	2 yds.
■ Red	#19	#02	2 yds.
▨ Royal	#09	#32	2 yds.
▨ Straw	#41	#19	2 yds.
▨ Silver	#40	#37	1½ yds.
▨ Dk. Brown	#36	#15	1 yd.
▨ Dk. Green	#31	#27	1 yd.
▨ Sail Blue	#04	#35	1 yd.

STITCH KEY:

— Backstitch/Straight Stitch
● French Knot

A – Dracula Coaster
(cut 1) 25 x 25 holes

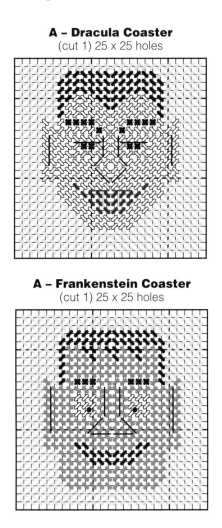

A – Frankenstein Coaster
(cut 1) 25 x 25 holes

A – Jack-o-Lantern Coaster
(cut 1) 25 x 25 holes

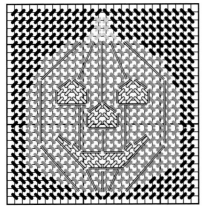

A – Skull Coaster
(cut 1) 25 x 25 holes

A – Graveyard Coaster
(cut 1) 25 x 25 holes

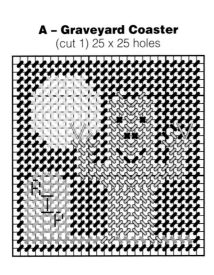

A – Ghost Coaster
(cut 1) 25 x 25 holes

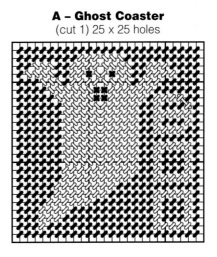

A – Witch Coaster
(cut 1) 25 x 25 holes

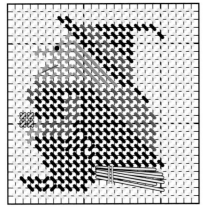

A – Scarecrow Coaster
(cut 1) 25 x 25 holes

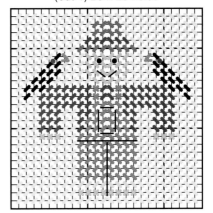

Pumpkin Patch

Designed by Gina Woods

SIZE: 4¼" x 10" x 6½" tall.

MATERIALS: One sheet of clear stiff 7-count plastic canvas; ½ sheet of black 7-count plastic canvas; Scraps of orange 7-count and clear 14-count plastic canvas; One green and two lt. green 12" chenille stems; Two brown 8-mm faceted beads; Craft glue or glue gun; Six-strand embroidery floss (for amounts see Color Key); Worsted-weight or plastic canvas yarn (for amounts see Color Key).

CUTTING INSTRUCTIONS:

NOTE: Graphs continued on page 122.

A: For back, cut one from stiff according to graph.
B: For bottom, cut one from stiff 24 x 60 holes.
C: For shutters, cut four from stiff according to graph.
D: For porch cover, cut one from stiff according to graph.
E: For stem, cut one from stiff according to graph.
F: For ghosts, cut two from stiff according to graph.
G: For leaves, cut eight from stiff according to graph.
H: For top window, cut one from orange according to graph.
I: For bottom windows, cut two from orange according to graph.
J: For fence front, cut one from black according to graph.
K: For fence sides, cut two from black according to graph.
L: For sign, cut one from 14-count 9 x 12 holes.

STITCHING INSTRUCTIONS:

1: Using yarn colors indicated and Continental Stitch, work A-E (two C on opposite side of canvas) pieces according to graphs; using white and Continental Stitch,

work F pieces on opposite sides of canvas. Using dk. green and stitches indicated, work three G pieces according to graph; substituting lime for dk. green, work remaining G pieces according to graph. With matching colors, Overcast unfinished edges of D-G pieces.

2: Using six strands tan floss and Continental Stitch, work L; Overcast unfinished edges. Using six strands black floss, Backstitch and Straight Stitch, embroider facial detail and letters on F and L pieces as indicated on graphs.

3: Holding H to right side of A, with dk. orange, Whipstitch outer edges of H to cutout edges at top of A; repeat with each I and each lower window cutout.

4: Using yarn colors indicated, Backstitch, Straight Stitch and Lazy Daisy Stitch, embroider detail as indicated on A-C graphs. With tan, Whipstitch one C to each unworked area on A as indicated on graphs; Overcast unfinished edges of shutters.

5: Omitting front corners of fence, with tan, Whipstitch A, B, J and K pieces together. With dk. orange for top of pumpkin as shown in photo and with tan, Overcast unfinished edges of back.

NOTE: Cut each color chenille stem into three or four different lengths.

6: Twist each chenille length around a pencil to curl. Glue two lt. green stems, one ghost and sign to fence; glue one bead to each corner fence post as shown. Glue remaining pieces to back as indicated and as shown.✧

E – Stem
(cut 1 from stiff)
7 x 9 holes

G – Leaf
(cut 8 from stiff)
7 x 8 holes

D – Porch Cover
(cut 1 from stiff)
6 x 17 holes
Glue to A.

F – Ghost
(cut 2 from stiff)
11 x 13 holes

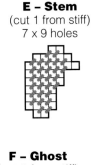

C – Shutter
(cut 4 from stiff)
3 x 6 holes

Whipstitch to A.

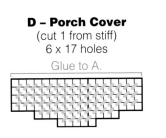

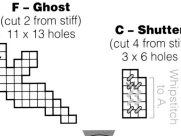

COLOR KEY: Pumpkin Patch

Embroidery floss			AMOUNT
■ Black			2 yds.
□ Tan			2 yds.

Worsted-weight	Nylon Plus™	Need-loft®	YARN AMOUNT
Orange	#17	#58	30 yds.
Tan	#33	#18	25 yds.
Lime	#29	#22	9 yds.
Camel	#34	#43	8 yds.
Cinnamon	#44	#14	8 yds.
Dk. Green	#31	#27	8 yds.
Dk. Orange	#18	#52	8 yds.
White	#01	#41	6 yds.
Black	#02	#00	1 yd.

STITCH KEY:
- — Backstitch/Straight Stitch
- ⌒ Lazy Daisy
- ☐ Unworked Area/Shutter Attachment
- — Porch Cover Placement

Pumpkin Patch

PHOTO ON PAGE 120

K – Fence Side
(cut 2 from black)
12 x 24 holes

Cut out gray areas carefully.

A – Back
(cut 1 from stiff)
35 x 60 holes

Cut Out

Cut Out

Cut Out

B – Bottom
(cut 1 from stiff) 24 x 60 holes

Whipstitch to A.

J – Fence Front
(cut 1 from black)
12 x 60 holes

Cut out gray areas carefully.

L – Sign
(cut 1 from 14-count)
9 x 12 holes

TRICK OR TREAT

H – Top Window
(cut 1 from orange)
8 x 8 holes

Cut out gray areas carefully.

I – Bottom Window
(cut 2 from orange)
6 x 7 holes

Cut out gray areas carefully.

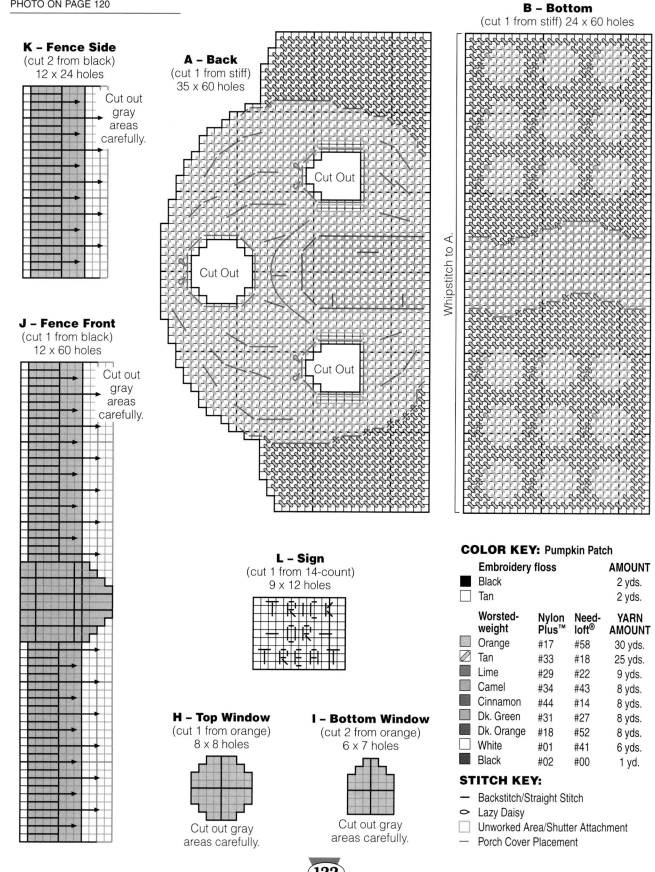

COLOR KEY: Pumpkin Patch

Embroidery floss			AMOUNT
■ Black			2 yds.
□ Tan			2 yds.

Worsted-weight	Nylon Plus™	Need-loft®	YARN AMOUNT
Orange	#17	#58	30 yds.
Tan	#33	#18	25 yds.
Lime	#29	#22	9 yds.
Camel	#34	#43	8 yds.
Cinnamon	#44	#14	8 yds.
Dk. Green	#31	#27	8 yds.
Dk. Orange	#18	#52	8 yds.
White	#01	#41	6 yds.
Black	#02	#00	1 yd.

STITCH KEY:

— Backstitch/Straight Stitch
○ Lazy Daisy
☐ Unworked Area/Shutter Attachment
— Porch Cover Placement

Midnight Mobile

Designed by Trudy Bath Smith

SIZE: Cat is 9" x 9½".

MATERIALS: 1½ sheets of black 7-count plastic canvas; One sheet each of neon yellow, purple and glow-in-the-dark 7-count plastic canvas; One silver 22-mm jingle bell; Metallic cord (for amounts see Color Key).

CUTTING INSTRUCTIONS:

A: For cat body, cut two from black according to graph.

B: For cat head, cut two from black according to graph.

C: For cat eyes, cut four from yellow according to graph.

D: For moon pieces #1 and #2, cut one #1 from yellow and one #2 from glow-in-the-dark according to graphs.

E: For large star pieces #1 and #2, cut three #1 from yellow and three #2 from glow-in-the-dark according to graphs.

F: For small star pieces #1 and #2, cut three #1 and three #2 from purple according to graphs.

G: For collar, cut one from purple 3 x 22 holes.

STITCHING INSTRUCTIONS:

NOTE: D-F pieces are unworked.

1: Using white/silver and stitches indicated, work A (one on opposite side of canvas) and B pieces according to graphs. Using white/silver and stitches indicated, work G according to graph, threading bell on center stitch as you work.

2: To attach each eye, holding one C behind one cutout on A at matching edges, using

Midnight Mobile

PHOTO ON PAGE 123

black/silver and stitches indicated, work through both thicknesses as one according to A graph.

3: Holding A pieces wrong sides together, with black/silver, Whipstitch together. Wrapping collar around front leg as shown in photo, Whipstitch ends to body through all thicknesses as indicated.

4: Holding B pieces wrong sides together (slide lower section over body as indicated), Whipstitch together, working through all thicknesses at head attachment area.

5: Slide D pieces together at slots; with black/silver, Overcast outside edges, tacking pieces together as you work to secure. Join moon to tail

by securing a length of black/silver under stitches on each piece as shown. For hanger, attach a length of black/silver to top edge of moon as shown; form loop at opposite end.

6: For each large star, slide one of each E piece together at slots. With black/silver, Overcast outer edges, tacking pieces together at top and bottom as you work to secure. For each small star, slide one of each F piece together.

NOTE: Cut one 7", one 13" and one 20" length of black/silver.

7: For each star streamer, assemble one cut strand of cord and one of each size star according to Streamer Assembly Diagram; secure end of cords to bottom edge of body as shown. ✧

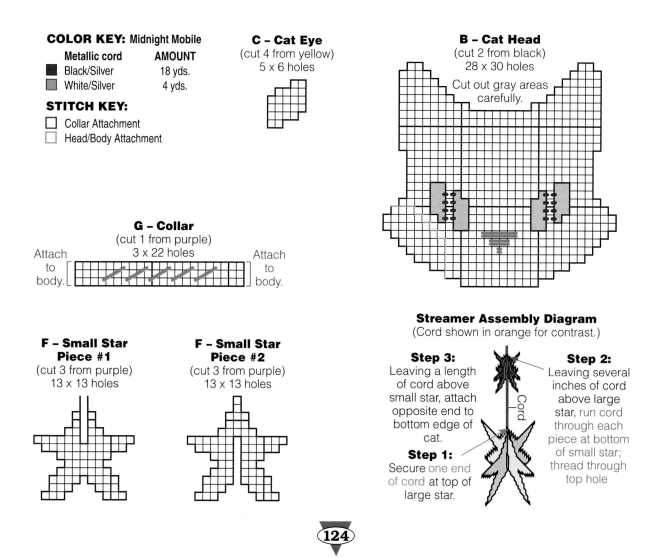

COLOR KEY: Midnight Mobile

Metallic cord	AMOUNT
■ Black/Silver	18 yds.
▨ White/Silver	4 yds.

STITCH KEY:
- ☐ Collar Attachment
- ☐ Head/Body Attachment

C – Cat Eye
(cut 4 from yellow)
5 x 6 holes

B – Cat Head
(cut 2 from black)
28 x 30 holes
Cut out gray areas carefully.

G – Collar
(cut 1 from purple)
3 x 22 holes
Attach to body. — Attach to body.

F – Small Star Piece #1
(cut 3 from purple)
13 x 13 holes

F – Small Star Piece #2
(cut 3 from purple)
13 x 13 holes

Streamer Assembly Diagram
(Cord shown in orange for contrast.)

Step 3: Leaving a length of cord above small star, attach opposite end to bottom edge of cat.

Step 2: Leaving several inches of cord above large star, run cord through each piece at bottom of small star; thread through top hole

Step 1: Secure one end of cord at top of large star.

Cord

E – Large Star Piece #1
(cut 3 from yellow)
26 x 27 holes

A – Cat Body
(cut 2 from black)
42 x 62 holes

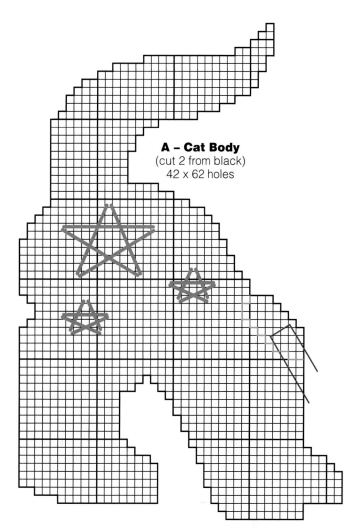

E – Large Star Piece #2
(cut 3 from glow-in-the-dark)
26 x 27 holes

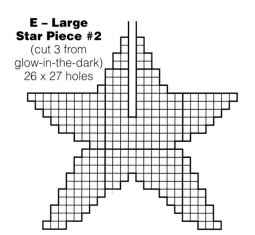

Cut through bars carefully.

D – Moon Piece #1
(cut 1 from yellow)
33 x 33 holes

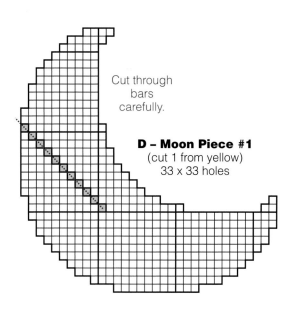

D – Moon Piece #2
(cut 1 from glow-in-the-dark)
33 x 33 holes

Cut through bars carefully.

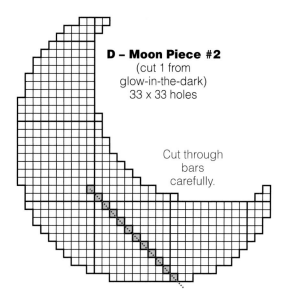

Every Day's a Holiday

From harvest
feast to Easter egg
hunt, the changing seasons
inspire our holiday celebrations.
And what better way to bring family
and friends together than to reflect those
seasonal changes in our daily lives?
Involve your family in cutting and
stitching these festive, all-seasons
projects, and give your
home a holiday
atmosphere
year round.

Cone Ornaments

Designed by Dianne Davis

SIZE: Each is about 2½" across x 3".

MATERIALS: Four 6" plastic canvas radial circles; One 3" plastic canvas radial circle; One each green and white 4" chenille stem; One gold ⅝" star sequin; 16 red star sequins; ¼ yd. green ⅛" satin ribbon; 4" x 6" piece each of black, white, red and green felt; One each white and black 13-mm pom-pom and one white 5-mm pom-pom; One pair 4-mm wiggle eyes; Three silver 6-mm jingle bells; Craft glue or glue gun; Six-strand embroidery floss (for amounts see Color Key on page 130); Worsted-weight or plastic canvas yarn (for amounts see Color Key).

CUTTING INSTRUCTIONS:

NOTE: Graphs on pages 130 & 131.

A: For Ornaments, cut one from each 6" circle according to graphs.

B: For pumpkin, cut one from 3" circle according to graph.

C: For linings, using one A piece as a pattern, cut one from each color felt.

STITCHING INSTRUCTIONS:

1: Using colors and stitches indicated, work A and B pieces according to graphs; with dk. orange, Overcast edges of B.

2: Using six strands floss in colors indicated, Backstitch, Fly Stitch and French Knot, embroider facial detail as indicated on A and B graphs. Using two strands black floss and Backstitch, embroider hat detail as indicated on Santa A graph. Using yarn colors indicated and Modified Turkey Work Stitch (leave 1" loops for Witch and ½" loops for Santa) embroider hair as indicated on Witch and Santa A graphs; cut loops and fray ends.

3: For each Ornament, overlapping one A piece two holes (straight edge over ragged edge) and working through both thicknesses at overlap areas to join, with matching color, Whipstitch together, forming cone; Overcast unfinished edges.

NOTE: Cut eight 2" lengths of black floss. Cut white chenille stem in half.

4: For spider, glue eyes and floss strands to black pom-pom (see photo). For Ghost, insert white 13-mm pom-pom from inside into opening at top of cone (see photo); glue to secure. Insert one end of each chenille piece into one cutout, forming arms; glue to secure and shape as desired. Glue spider to arms as shown in photo. Glue white felt lining C to inside of cone.

NOTE: Cut two 1" lengths of lt. green and one 1" length of dk. orange.

5: For Witch, cut two sleeves from black felt according to Sleeve Cutting Diagram. Thread ends of 1" dk. orange strand from front to back through holes at top of B, forming a loop (see photo); glue to secure. Thread lt. green strands through loop of pumpkin; for each hand, glue ends of one lt. green strand to cuff edge of one sleeve as shown. Glue assembly to front of Witch as shown. Glue black felt lining C to inside of cone.

NOTE: Cut green chenille stem in half.

6: For Tree, insert one end of each green chenille piece into one cutout, forming arms; glue to secure and shape as desired. Glue green felt lining C to inside of cone. Glue sequins to Tree as shown or as desired.

7: For Santa, cut two sleeves from red felt according to Sleeve Cutting Diagram on page 131. Tie green ribbon into a bow; trim ends. Glue bow, 5-mm pom-pom, sleeves and bells to Santa as shown. Glue red felt lining C to inside of cone.

NOTES: Cut one 16" length each of white, black, green and red. Cut two 9" lengths each of black, orange, red and green floss.

For shoe pieces, cut four from each color felt according to Shoe Piece Cutting Diagram on page 131.

CONTINUED ON PAGE 130

128

Cone Ornaments

CONTINUED FROM PAGE 128

8: For hanger/legs on each Ornament, fold matching color 16" strand in half and tie a knot, leaving a 3" loop. Thread ends from outside to inside through top of cone; cut each end ¾" below bottom edge of cone. For each shoe, holding two matching color shoe pieces together with one end of yarn strand between, glue together.

For each shoelace, thread one 9" strand floss (black for Ghost, orange for Witch, red for Tree and green for Santa) through each shoe as indicated on Shoe Cutting Diagram and tie into a bow; trim ends.✧

COLOR KEY: Cone Ornaments

Embroidery floss			AMOUNT
■ Black			2½ yds.
☐ Orange			1 yd.
▨ Lt. Green			½ yd.
☐ Green			½ yd.
☐ Red			½ yd.

Worsted-weight	Nylon Plus™	Need-loft®	YARN AMOUNT
▨ White	#01	#41	10 yds.
▨ Red	#19	#02	9 yds.
▨ Dk. Green	#31	#27	8 yds.
■ Black	#02	#00	8½ yds.
▨ Gray	#23	#38	2 yds.
▨ Dk. Orange	#18	#52	1 yd.
▨ Lt. Green	#28	#26	1 yd.
▨ Pink	#11	#07	½ yd.

STITCH KEY:

— Backstitch/Straight Stitch
● French Knot
⌇ Modified Turkey Work Stitch
Y Fly Stitch
✦ Shoelace Attachment

A – Ghost
(cut 1 from 6" circle)
Cut away gray area.

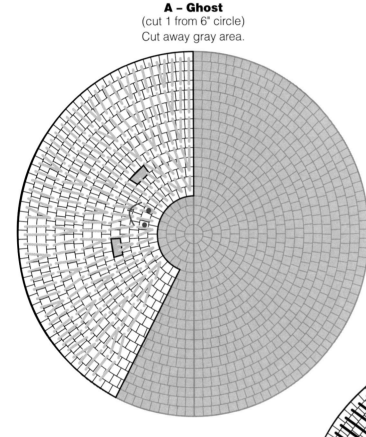

A – Witch
(cut 1 from 6" circle)
Cut away gray area.

B – Pumpkin
(cut 1 from 3" circle)
Cut away gray area.

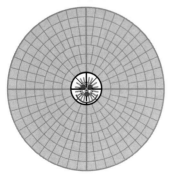

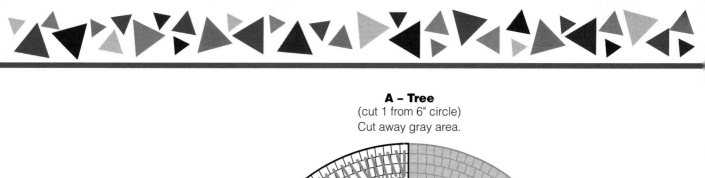

A – Tree
(cut 1 from 6" circle)
Cut away gray area.

**Sleeve Cutting
Diagram**
(actual size)

Cuff Edge

**Shoe Piece
Cutting Diagram**
(actual size)

A – Santa
(cut 1 from 6" circle)
Cut away gray area.

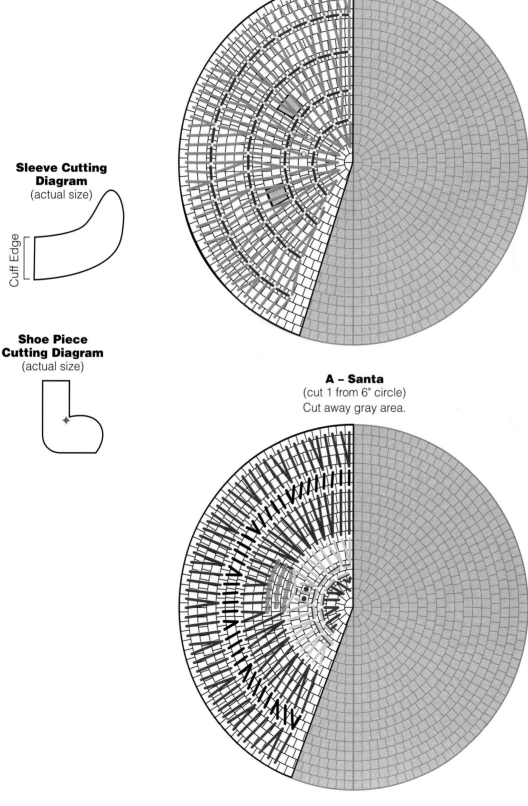

Time to Celebrate

Designed by Cherie Marie Leck

Interchange these festive motifs at holiday time.

SIZE: Clock is 1¼" x 8⅜" x 12".

MATERIALS: One sheet of stiff 12" x 18" or larger 7-count plastic canvas; Three sheets of regular-flexibility 12" x 18" or larger 7-count plastic canvas; Standard quartz clock movement (⅜" shaft) with hands; 24" Velcro® closure strip; Sewing needle and white thread; Metallic cord (for amounts see Clock, Winter, Spring and Summer Color Keys on pages 135-137); Worsted-weight or plastic canvas yarn (for amounts see individual Color Keys).

NOTES: Graphs on pages 134-137 & 141.

CUTTING INSTRUCTIONS:

Use stiff for A-D and regular flexibility canvas for remaining pieces.

A: For Clock front, cut one according to graph.

B: For Clock back, cut one from stiff 43 x 67 holes (no graph); cut out hanger and movement openings according to Clock Back Cutting Guide.

C: For Clock sides, cut two from stiff 7 x 67 holes (no graph).

D: For Clock top and bottom, cut two from stiff (one for top and one for bottom) 7 x 43 holes (no graph).

E: For winter tree, cut two according to graph.

F: For winter joy, cut two according to graph.

G: For winter love, cut two according to graph.

SPRING

H: For winter heart trio, cut two according to graph.

I: For spring shamrock, cut two according to graph.

J: For spring rainbow, cut two according to graph.

K: For spring flowers, cut two according to graph.

L: For spring chick and eggs, cut two according to graph.

M: For spring mom, cut two according to graph.

N: For summer star, cut two according to graph.

O: For summer dad, cut two according to graph.

P: For summer flag, cut two according to graph.

Q: For summer sea gull, cut two according to graph.

R: For summer lighthouse, cut two according to graph.

S: For fall bat, cut two according to graph.

T: For fall ghost, cut two according to graph.

U: For fall corn, cut two according to graph.

V: For fall pumpkin, cut two according to graph.

STITCHING INSTRUCTIONS:

NOTES: B and one of each E-V piece is

WINTER

Time To Celebrate

CONTINUED FROM PAGE 133

unworked. Cut Velcro® strip into eighteen 1-1¼" lengths.

1: For Clock, using eggshell and stitches indicated, work A according to graph; Overcast unfinished edges. Using eggshell and Long Stitch over narrow width, work C and D pieces. Using yellow/gold cord, Cross Stitch and French Knot, embroider clock face as indicated

FALL

on A graph. With thread, sew two loopy-side Velcro® pieces to A as indicated. Attach clock movement through cutout on A according to manufacturer's instructions; with eggshell, Whipstitch and assemble A-D pieces as indicated and according to Clock Assembly Diagram.

2: Using colors and stitches indicated, work one of each E-V piece according to graphs. Using yarn and cord in colors and stitches indicated, embroider detail as indicated.

SUMMER

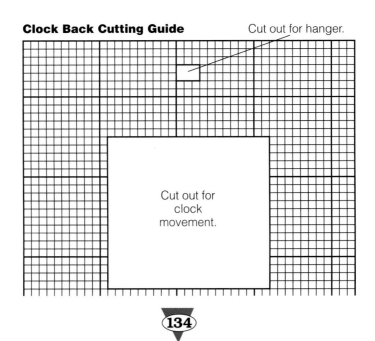

Clock Back Cutting Guide

Cut out for hanger.

Cut out for clock movement.

3: With thread, sew one fuzzy-side Velcro® piece to center of each unworked E-V piece.

4: For each motif, holding unworked piece Velcro® side out to wrong side of matching worked piece, with lt. pink for G, yellow/gold cord for I, silver cord for N, dk. royal for P, purple for S, black for ghost edges of T, maple for straw edges of V and with matching colors as shown in photo, Whipstitch together.

5: For bow on F, tie a strand of red into a bow; trim ends. Glue bow to bottom of F as shown.

6: For the months of December and January, display tree and joy on Clock. For remaining months, display as follows: February, love and heart trio; March, shamrock and rainbow; April, flowers and chick and eggs; May, flowers or heart trio and mom; June, heart trio or star and dad; July, star and flag; August and September, sea gull and lighthouse; October, bat and ghost; November, corn and pumpkin.✧

A – Clock Front
(cut 1 from stiff) 55 x 79 holes

Cut out gray area.

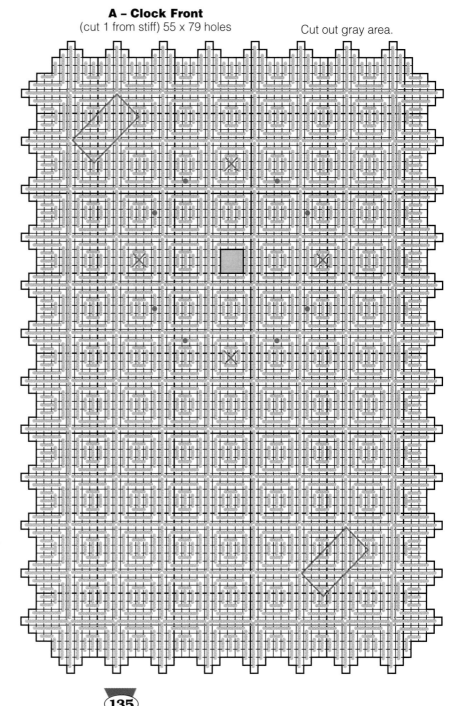

Clock Assembly Diagram
(back view)

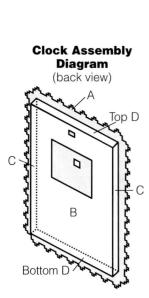

COLOR KEY: Clock

Metallic cord			AMOUNT
Yellow/Gold			2 yds.

Worsted-weight	Nylon Plus™	Need-loft®	YARN AMOUNT
Eggshell	#24	#39	40 yds.

STITCH KEY:
- • French Knot
- × Cross Stitch
- □ Clock Side, Top & Bottom Attachment
- □ Velcro® Attachment

Time To Celebrate

PHOTO ON PAGES 132 & 133

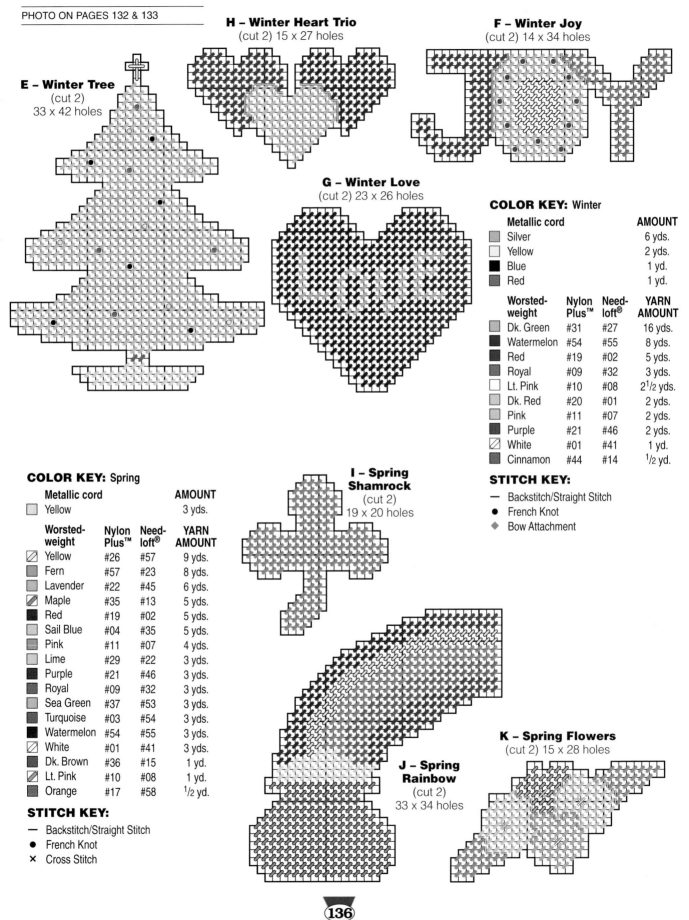

H – Winter Heart Trio
(cut 2) 15 x 27 holes

F – Winter Joy
(cut 2) 14 x 34 holes

E – Winter Tree
(cut 2)
33 x 42 holes

G – Winter Love
(cut 2) 23 x 26 holes

I – Spring Shamrock
(cut 2)
19 x 20 holes

J – Spring Rainbow
(cut 2)
33 x 34 holes

K – Spring Flowers
(cut 2) 15 x 28 holes

COLOR KEY: Winter

Metallic cord			AMOUNT
Silver			6 yds.
Yellow			2 yds.
Blue			1 yd.
Red			1 yd.

Worsted-weight	Nylon Plus™	Need-loft®	YARN AMOUNT
Dk. Green	#31	#27	16 yds.
Watermelon	#54	#55	8 yds.
Red	#19	#02	5 yds.
Royal	#09	#32	3 yds.
Lt. Pink	#10	#08	2$\frac{1}{2}$ yds.
Dk. Red	#20	#01	2 yds.
Pink	#11	#07	2 yds.
Purple	#21	#46	2 yds.
White	#01	#41	1 yd.
Cinnamon	#44	#14	$\frac{1}{2}$ yd.

STITCH KEY:
— Backstitch/Straight Stitch
● French Knot
◆ Bow Attachment

COLOR KEY: Spring

Metallic cord			AMOUNT
Yellow			3 yds.

Worsted-weight	Nylon Plus™	Need-loft®	YARN AMOUNT
Yellow	#26	#57	9 yds.
Fern	#57	#23	8 yds.
Lavender	#22	#45	6 yds.
Maple	#35	#13	5 yds.
Red	#19	#02	5 yds.
Sail Blue	#04	#35	5 yds.
Pink	#11	#07	4 yds.
Lime	#29	#22	3 yds.
Purple	#21	#46	3 yds.
Royal	#09	#32	3 yds.
Sea Green	#37	#53	3 yds.
Turquoise	#03	#54	3 yds.
Watermelon	#54	#55	3 yds.
White	#01	#41	3 yds.
Dk. Brown	#36	#15	1 yd.
Lt. Pink	#10	#08	1 yd.
Orange	#17	#58	$\frac{1}{2}$ yd.

STITCH KEY:
— Backstitch/Straight Stitch
● French Knot
× Cross Stitch

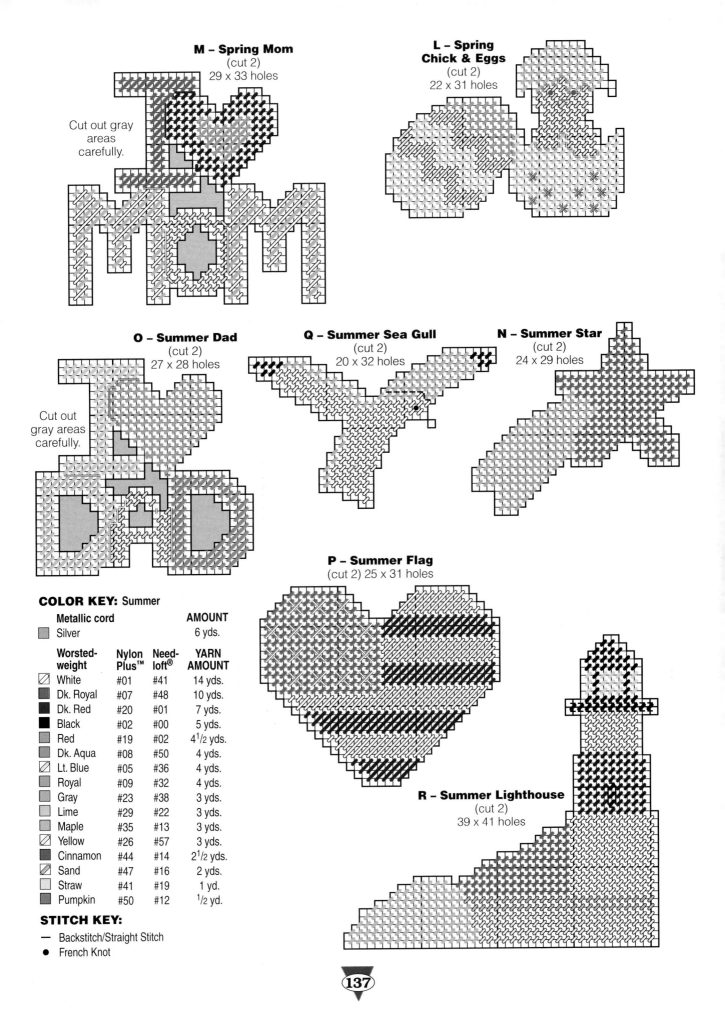

M – Spring Mom
(cut 2)
29 x 33 holes

Cut out gray areas carefully.

L – Spring Chick & Eggs
(cut 2)
22 x 31 holes

O – Summer Dad
(cut 2)
27 x 28 holes

Cut out gray areas carefully.

Q – Summer Sea Gull
(cut 2)
20 x 32 holes

N – Summer Star
(cut 2)
24 x 29 holes

P – Summer Flag
(cut 2) 25 x 31 holes

R – Summer Lighthouse
(cut 2)
39 x 41 holes

COLOR KEY: Summer

	Metallic cord			AMOUNT
	Silver			6 yds.

	Worsted-weight	Nylon Plus™	Need-loft®	YARN AMOUNT
	White	#01	#41	14 yds.
	Dk. Royal	#07	#48	10 yds.
	Dk. Red	#20	#01	7 yds.
	Black	#02	#00	5 yds.
	Red	#19	#02	4½ yds.
	Dk. Aqua	#08	#50	4 yds.
	Lt. Blue	#05	#36	4 yds.
	Royal	#09	#32	4 yds.
	Gray	#23	#38	3 yds.
	Lime	#29	#22	3 yds.
	Maple	#35	#13	3 yds.
	Yellow	#26	#57	3 yds.
	Cinnamon	#44	#14	2½ yds.
	Sand	#47	#16	2 yds.
	Straw	#41	#19	1 yd.
	Pumpkin	#50	#12	½ yd.

STITCH KEY:

— Backstitch/Straight Stitch

● French Knot

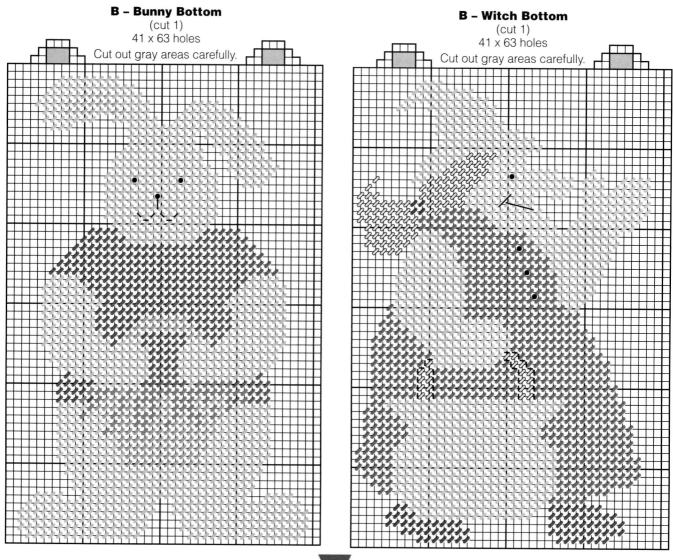

Seasonal Welcome

Designed by Michele Wilcox

SIZE: 10¼" x about 14½".

MATERIALS: 2½ sheets of 7-count plastic canvas; 1 yd. white ¼" satin ribbon; #3 pearl cotton (for amounts see Color Key); Worsted-weight or plastic canvas yarn (for amounts see Color Key).

CONTINUED ON PAGE 140

COLOR KEY: Seasonal Welcome

#3 pearl cotton			AMOUNT
Black			4 yds.
Blue			¼ yd.
Red			¼ yd.

Worsted-weight	Nylon Plus™	Need-loft®	YARN AMOUNT
White	#01	#41	55 yds.
Tangerine	#15	#11	23 yds.
Lt. Green	#28	#26	20 yds.
Crimson	#53	#42	18 yds.
Denim	#06	#33	18 yds.
Maple	#35	#13	16 yds.
Plum	#55	#59	16 yds.
Black	#02	#00	15 yds.
Gray	#23	#38	10 yds.
Camel	#34	#43	9 yds.
Mint	#30	#24	5 yds.
Dk. Green	#31	#27	4 yds.
Dk. Orange	#18	#52	3 yds.
Flesh	#14	#56	3 yds.
Royal	#09	#32	3 yds.
Cinnamon	#44	#14	1 yd.

STITCH KEY:

— Backstitch/Straight Stitch
● French Knot

B – Bunny Bottom
(cut 1)
41 x 63 holes
Cut out gray areas carefully.

B – Witch Bottom
(cut 1)
41 x 63 holes
Cut out gray areas carefully.

Seasonal Welcome

CONTINUED FROM PAGE 138

CUTTING INSTRUCTIONS:

A: For top, cut one according to graph.

B: For bottoms, cut one each according to graphs.

STITCHING INSTRUCTIONS:

NOTE: Use Continental Stitch throughout.

1: Using colors indicated, work pieces according to graphs; fill in uncoded areas using lt. green for Bunny, maple for Pilgrim, denim for Santa and tangerine for Witch. With background color,

Overcast edges.

2: Using colors indicated, Backstitch, Straight Stitch and French Knot, embroider facial and caldron handle detail and Witch dress buttons as indicated on B graphs.

NOTE: Cut ribbon in half.

3: With Lark's Head Knot, attach one ribbon to each small cutout on sign top (see photo); attach one sign bottom with bows as shown. Hang as desired. ✧

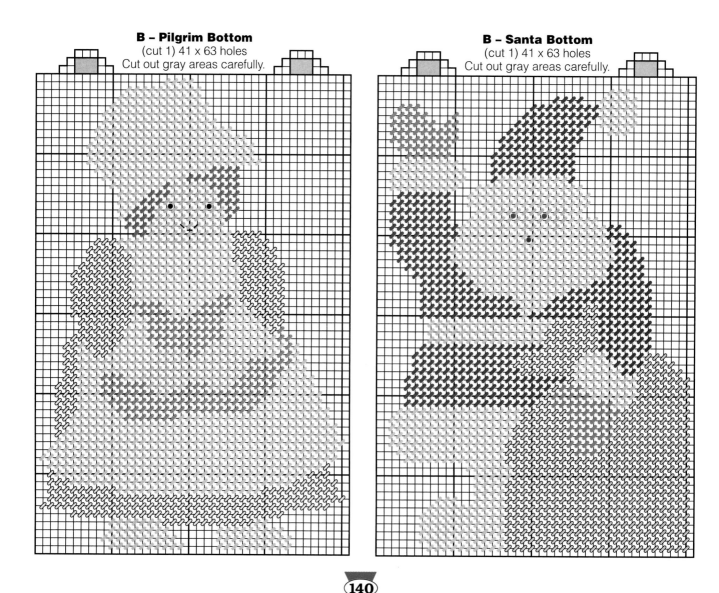

B – Pilgrim Bottom
(cut 1) 41 x 63 holes
Cut out gray areas carefully.

B – Santa Bottom
(cut 1) 41 x 63 holes
Cut out gray areas carefully.

COLOR KEY: Seasonal Welcome

#3 pearl cotton	AMOUNT
Black	4 yds.
Blue	1/4 yd.
Red	1/4 yd.

Worsted-weight	Nylon Plus™	Need-loft®	YARN AMOUNT
White	#01	#41	55 yds.
Tangerine	#15	#11	23 yds.

Lt. Green	#28	#26	20 yds.
Crimson	#53	#42	18 yds.
Denim	#06	#33	18 yds.
Maple	#35	#13	16 yds.
Plum	#55	#59	16 yds.
Black	#02	#00	15 yds.
Gray	#23	#38	10 yds.
Camel	#34	#43	9 yds.
Mint	#30	#24	5 yds.

Dk. Green	#31	#27	4 yds.
Dk. Orange	#18	#52	3 yds.
Flesh	#14	#56	3 yds.
Royal	#09	#32	3 yds.
Cinnamon	#44	#14	1 yd.

STITCH KEY:
- — Backstitch/Straight Stitch
- ● French Knot

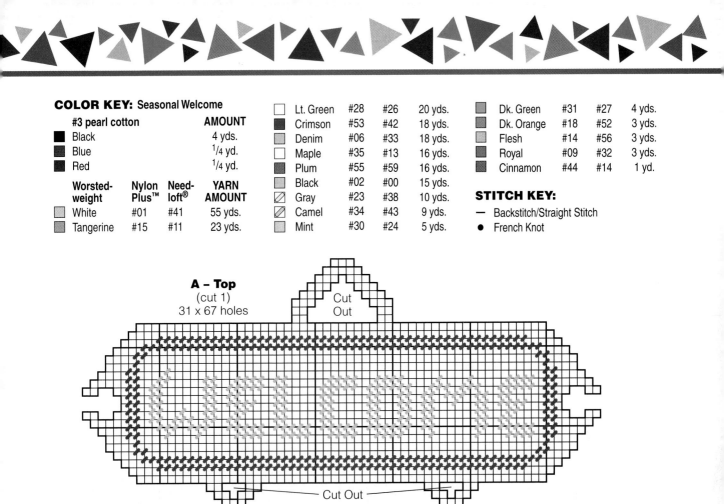

A – Top
(cut 1)
31 x 67 holes

Cut Out

Cut Out

Time To Celebrate

PHOTO ON PAGE 132

S – Fall Bat
(cut 2) 11 x 27 holes

V – Fall Pumpkin
(cut 2) 21 x 31 holes

T – Fall Ghost
(cut 2)
23 x 24 holes

U – Fall Corn
(cut 2)
22 x 25 holes

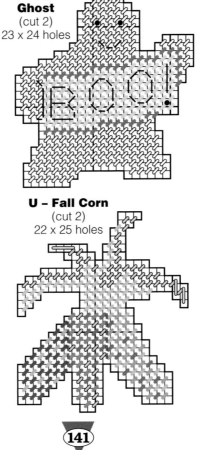

COLOR KEY: Fall

Worsted-weight	Nylon Plus™	Need-loft®	YARN AMOUNT
Black	#02	#00	6 yds.
Pumpkin	#50	#12	6 yds.
White	#01	#41	5 yds.
Dk. Orange	#18	#52	4 yds.
Camel	#34	#43	3 yds.
Dk. Brown	#36	#15	3 yds.
Tan	#33	#18	3 yds.
Yellow	#26	#57	3 yds.
Beige	#43	#40	2 yds.
Maple	#35	#13	2 yds.
Orange	#17	#58	2 yds.
Purple	#21	#46	2 yds.
Burgundy	#13	#03	1 yd.
Dk. Rust	#16	#10	1 yd.
Dusty Rose	#52	#06	1 yd.
Eggshell	#24	#39	1 yd.
Fern	#57	#23	1 yd.
Gold	#27	#17	1 yd.
Silver	#40	#37	1 yd.

STITCH KEY:
- — Backstitch/Straight Stitch
- ● French Knot

Holiday Holders

Designed by Debbie Tabor

SIZE: Thankful Turkey is 6" x 9" x 10" tall; Halloween Howler is 5½" x 8½" x 9¾" tall; Easter Bunny is 6" x 7½" x 12" tall.

MATERIALS FOR ONE: 2½ sheets of 7-count plastic canvas; Six-strand embroidery floss (for amounts see individual Color Keys on pages 144-146); Worsted-weight or plastic canvas yarn (for amounts see individual Color Keys).

NOTE: Graphs on pages 144-147.

THANKFUL TURKEY BASKET

CUTTING INSTRUCTIONS:

A: For body, cut one according to graph.
B: For wings, cut two according to graph.
C: For basket, cut one according to graph.
D: For basket base, cut one according to graph.

STITCHING INSTRUCTIONS:

1: Using colors indicated and Continental Stitch, work A, B (one on opposite side of canvas), C and D (leave uncoded area unworked) pieces according to graphs; fill in uncoded areas of A-C pieces using camel and Continental Stitch.

2: Holding edges right sides together, with camel, Whipstitch X edges of A together as indicated on graph. Holding edges wrong sides together, with matching colors, Whipstitch X edges of C together as indicated. With matching colors as shown in photo, Overcast edges of A-D pieces as indicated.

3: Using yarn and six strands floss in colors indicated, Backstitch and French Knot, embroider detail on A and C pieces as indicated.

4: With camel, Whipstitch B pieces to A as indicated. With camel, Whipstitch A and C pieces together as indicated; with yellow, Whipstitch body/basket assembly to D as indicated.

5: Soften wing tips with a blow-dry hair dryer set on low heat. Fold wings over edges of basket as shown; with camel, tack folded wings to basket sides as shown.

HALLOWEEN HOWLER BASKET

CUTTING INSTRUCTIONS:

A: For body, cut one according to graph.
B: For paws, cut two according to graph.
C: For basket, cut one according to graph.
D: For basket base, cut one according to graph.
E: For leaf, cut one according to graph.

STITCHING INSTRUCTIONS:

1: Using colors and stitches indicated, work A, C, D (leave uncoded area unworked) and E pieces according to graphs; fill in uncoded areas of A and work B pieces on opposite sides of canvas using black and Continental Stitch.

2: Holding edges wrong sides together, with dk. orange, Whipstitch X edges of C together as indicated on graph. For each bend in each leaf, holding edges right sides together, with green, tightly Whipstitch each cutout area of D and E pieces together according to Dart Illustration on page 144. With black for ears and with matching colors as shown in photo, Overcast edges of A-E pieces as indicated.

3: Using six strands floss in colors indicated, Backstitch and French Knot, embroider detail on A-C (reverse pattern on one B) pieces as indicated.

4: With black, Whipstitch A and B pieces together as indicated. With dk. orange, Whipstitch A and C pieces together as indicated; with green, Whipstitch body/basket assembly to D as indicated. With green, tack one end of E to center bottom of base. With black, tack paws to basket sides as shown.

EASTER BUNNY BASKET

CUTTING INSTRUCTIONS:

A: For body, cut one according to graph.
B: For paws, cut two according to graph.
C: For basket, cut one according to graph.
D: For basket base, cut one according to graph.

STITCHING INSTRUCTIONS:

NOTE: D piece is unworked.

1: Using colors and stitches indicated, work A and C pieces according to graphs; fill in uncoded areas of A and work B pieces on opposite sides of canvas using white and Continental Stitch.

2: Holding edges wrong sides together, with matching colors, Whipstitch X edges of C

Holiday Holders

CONTINUED FROM PAGE 143

together as indicated on graph. With matching colors as shown in photo, Overcast edges of A-C pieces as indicated.

3: Using six strands floss in colors indicated, Backstitch and French Knot, embroider detail on A-C (reverse pattern on one B) pieces as indicated.

4: With white, Whipstitch B pieces to A as indicated. With white, Whipstitch A and C pieces together as indicated; with lavender, Whipstitch body/basket assembly to D as indicated. With white, tack paws to basket sides as shown.✧

E – Halloween Howler Leaf
(cut 1) 15 x 29 holes

Cut out gray areas carefully.

COLOR KEY: Easter Bunny

Embroidery floss			AMOUNT
■ Black			6 yds.
■ White			½ yd.

Worsted-weight	Nylon Plus™	Need-loft®	YARN AMOUNT
□ Eggshell	#24	#39	44 yds.
▧ Lt. Blue	#05	#36	11 yds.
▧ Lavender	#22	#45	9 yds.
▨ Dk. Fuchsia			8 yds.
▨ Bt. Green		#61	7 yds.
■ Orange	#17	#58	6 yds.
■ Watermelon	#54	#55	4 yds.
▨ Pink	#11	#07	2 yds.
▧ White	#01	#41	1½ yds.
▧ Dk. Aqua	#08	#50	1 yd.
■ Black	#02	#00	½ yd.

STITCH KEY:

— Backstitch/Straight Stitch

● French Knot

□ Unworked Area/Basket Attachment

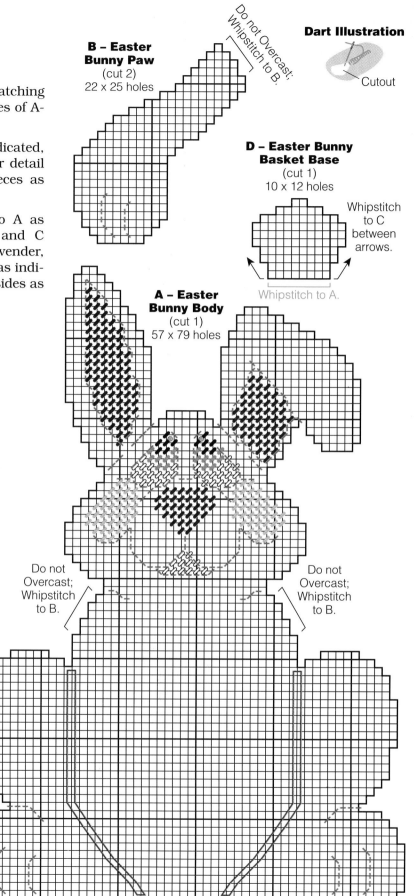

B – Easter Bunny Paw
(cut 2)
22 x 25 holes

Do not Overcast; Whipstitch to B.

Dart Illustration

Cutout

D – Easter Bunny Basket Base
(cut 1)
10 x 12 holes

Whipstitch to C between arrows.

Whipstitch to A.

A – Easter Bunny Body
(cut 1)
57 x 79 holes

Do not Overcast; Whipstitch to B.

Do not Overcast; Whipstitch to B.

Do not Overcast; Whipstitch to D.

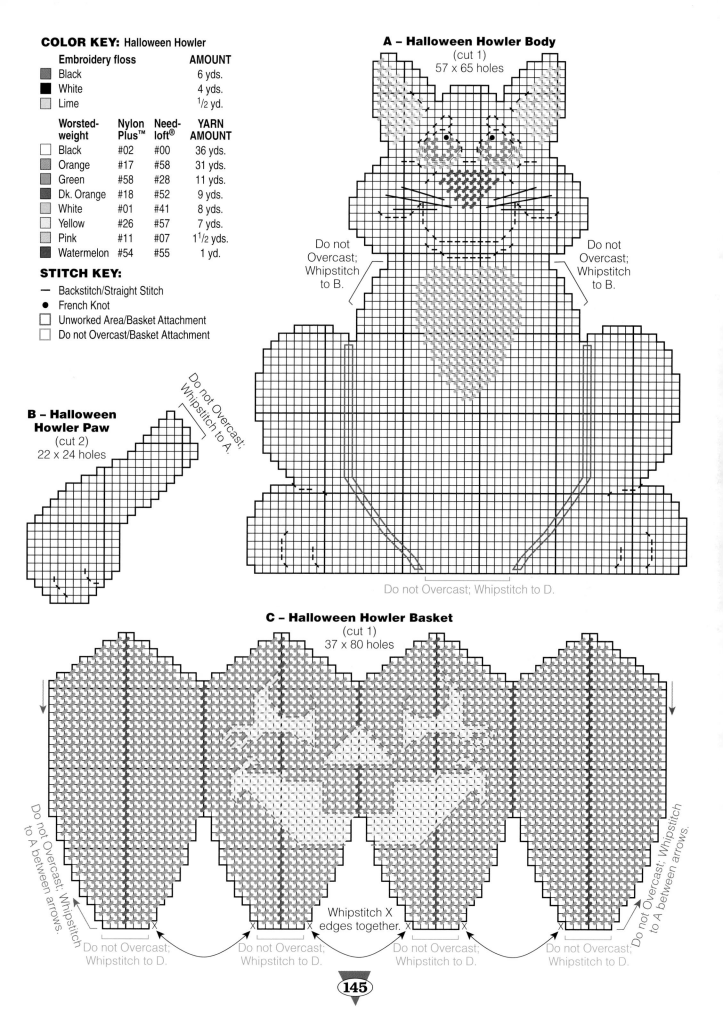

COLOR KEY: Halloween Howler

Embroidery floss	AMOUNT
Black	6 yds.
White	4 yds.
Lime	1/2 yd.

Worsted-weight	Nylon Plus™	Need-loft®	YARN AMOUNT
Black	#02	#00	36 yds.
Orange	#17	#58	31 yds.
Green	#58	#28	11 yds.
Dk. Orange	#18	#52	9 yds.
White	#01	#41	8 yds.
Yellow	#26	#57	7 yds.
Pink	#11	#07	1 1/2 yds.
Watermelon	#54	#55	1 yd.

STITCH KEY:

- — Backstitch/Straight Stitch
- • French Knot
- ☐ Unworked Area/Basket Attachment
- ☐ Do not Overcast/Basket Attachment

A – Halloween Howler Body
(cut 1)
57 x 65 holes

Do not Overcast; Whipstitch to B.

Do not Overcast; Whipstitch to B.

Do not Overcast; Whipstitch to D.

B – Halloween Howler Paw
(cut 2)
22 x 24 holes

Do not Overcast; Whipstitch to A.

C – Halloween Howler Basket
(cut 1)
37 x 80 holes

Do not Overcast; Whipstitch to A between arrows.

Do not Overcast; Whipstitch to A between arrows.

Whipstitch X edges together.

Do not Overcast; Whipstitch to D.

Do not Overcast; Whipstitch to D.

Do not Overcast; Whipstitch to D.

Do not Overcast; Whipstitch to D.

COLOR KEY: Thankful Turkey

Embroidery floss			AMOUNT
■ Black			15 yds.
■ Brown			5 yds.
▨ Lt. Brown			3 yds.
▨ Green			1½ yds.
■ Dk. Rust			1 yd.
▨ White			½ yd.

Worsted-weight	Nylon Plus™	Need-loft®	YARN AMOUNT
□ Camel	#34	#43	62 yds.
▨ Dk. Orange	#18	#52	10 yds.
▨ Orange	#17	#58	10 yds.
▨ Aqua	#60	#51	9 yds.
▨ Tangerine	#15	#11	9 yds.
▨ Bt. Green		#61	8 yds.
□ Dk. Brown	#36	#15	6 yds.
▨ Dk. Rust	#16	#10	6 yds.
▨ Red	#19	#02	6 yds.
▨ Purple	#21	#46	5 yds.
▨ Yellow	#26	#57	4 yds.
▨ Lemon	#25	#20	3 yds.
▨ Green	#58	#28	1½ yds.
▨ Sea Green	#37	#53	1½ yds.
▨ Black	#02	#00	1 yd.
▨ White	#01	#41	½ yd.

STITCH KEY:
- — Backstitch/Straight Stitch
- ● French Knot
- ☐ Unworked Area/Basket Attachment
- ☐ Unworked Area/Wing Attachment
- ⬚ Do Not Overcast/Basket Attachment

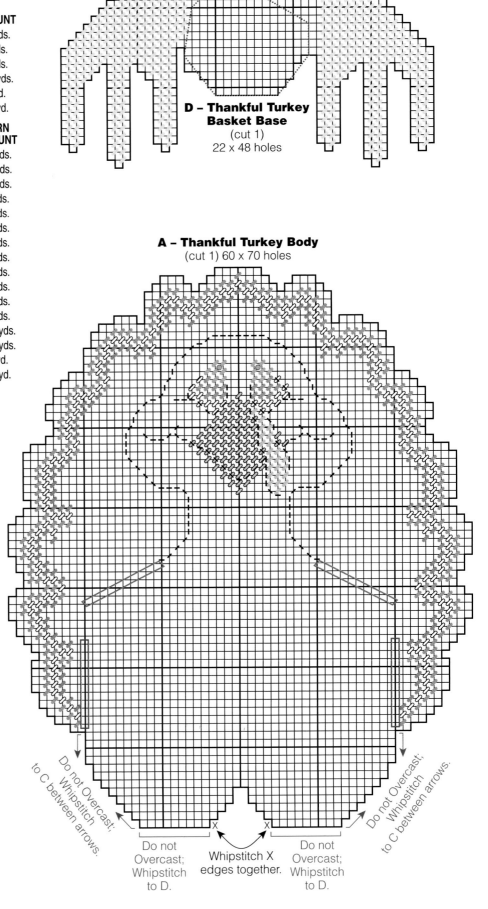

D – Thankful Turkey Basket Base
(cut 1)
22 x 48 holes

A – Thankful Turkey Body
(cut 1) 60 x 70 holes

Do not Overcast; Whipstitch to C between arrows.

Do not Overcast; Whipstitch to C between arrows.

Do not Overcast; Whipstitch to D.

Whipstitch X edges together.

Do not Overcast; Whipstitch to D.

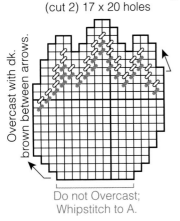

B – Thankful Turkey Wing
(cut 2) 17 x 20 holes

Overcast with dk. brown between arrows.

Do not Overcast; Whipstitch to A.

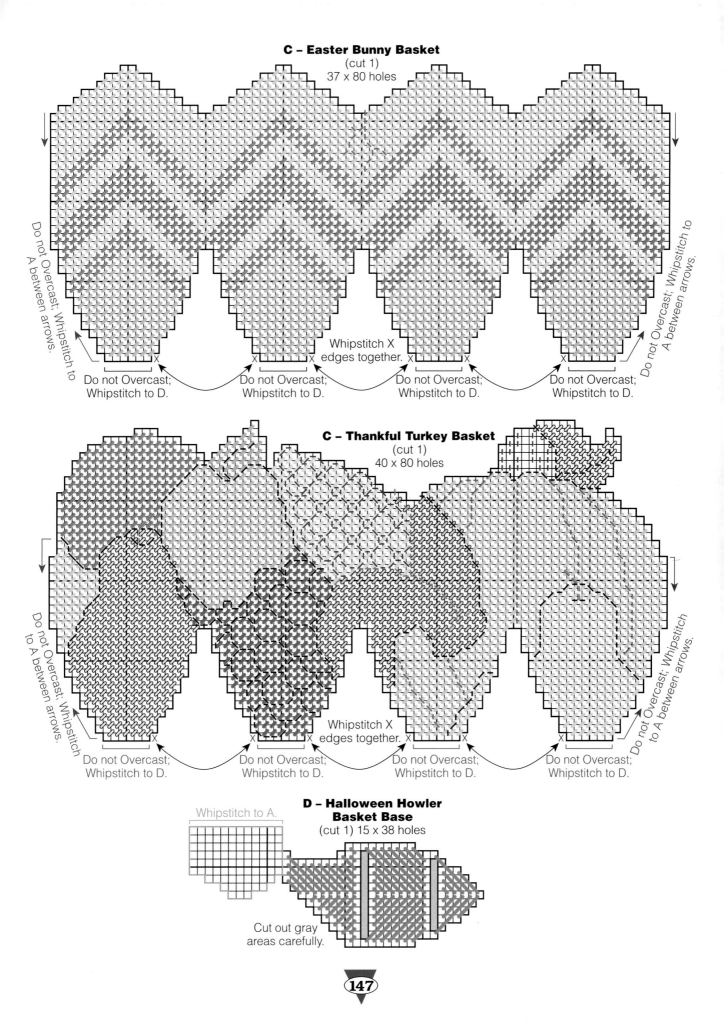

C – Easter Bunny Basket
(cut 1)
37 x 80 holes

Do not Overcast; Whipstitch to A between arrows.

Do not Overcast; Whipstitch to A between arrows.

Do not Overcast;
Whipstitch to D.

Do not Overcast;
Whipstitch to D.

Whipstitch X edges together.

Do not Overcast;
Whipstitch to D.

Do not Overcast;
Whipstitch to D.

C – Thankful Turkey Basket
(cut 1)
40 x 80 holes

Do not Overcast; Whipstitch to A between arrows.

Do not Overcast; Whipstitch to A between arrows.

Do not Overcast;
Whipstitch to D.

Do not Overcast;
Whipstitch to D.

Whipstitch X edges together.

Do not Overcast;
Whipstitch to D.

Do not Overcast;
Whipstitch to D.

D – Halloween Howler Basket Base
(cut 1) 15 x 38 holes

Whipstitch to A.

Cut out gray areas carefully.

Photo Hellos

Designed by Ruby Thacker

SIZE: Each "Boo" is 4" x 8½", each "Love" is 4½" x 12½", "Joy" is 4" x 7¼"; not including embellishments.

MATERIALS FOR ONE: ½ sheet of stiff 7-count plastic canvas; Scraps of black and green 7-count plastic canvas (for "BOO" and "JOY" respectively); 18 pairs of assorted-size wiggle eyes (for "Ghostly BOO"); One white 1" and four red ½" satin ribbon roses (for "Valentine LOVE"); 2-3 bunches of small flowers (for "Valentine LOVE"); ¾ yd. pink satin ribbon rose garland (for "Lattice LOVE"); Two red ½" round faceted acrylic stones (for "JOY"); Craft glue or glue gun; Metallic cord (for amounts see "JOY" Color Key on page 153); Worsted-weight or plastic canvas yarn (for amounts see individual Color Keys).

CUTTING INSTRUCTIONS:

NOTE: Graphs continued on pages 150 & 153.

A: For "LOVE" pieces, cut one each according to graphs.

B: For "BOO" pieces, cut number indicated according to graphs.

C: For "JOY" pieces, cut number indicated according to graphs.

STITCHING INSTRUCTIONS:

NOTE: Back and brace pieces are unworked.

1: For frame of choice, using colors and stitches indicated, work A pieces according to stitch pattern guide of choice; or, using white for "Ghostly BOO", orange for "Bat/Cat BOO" letters and black for cat and bat, white/gold for "JOY" letters and Continental Stitch and green and Long Stitch for "JOY" leaves, work B or C pieces. With matching colors, Overcast edges of cat and bat or leaves.

2: With camel for "Lattice LOVE", red for "Valentine LOVE", black for "BOO" or white/gold for "JOY", Overcast cutout edges of "O" pieces. Whipstitch brace to back as indicated on graphs. Holding back to wrong side of matching worked piece, omitting top edge of back, Whipstitch each letter together through all thicknesses as indicated; Overcast unfinished edges.

NOTE: From ribbon rose garland, cut two lengths of two or three roses.

3: Glue ribbon rose garland pieces to "Lattice LOVE", satin ribbon roses and small flowers to "Valentine LOVE", bat and cat to "Bat/Cat BOO", wiggle eyes to "Ghostly BOO", or leaves and stones to "JOY" as shown in photo.✧

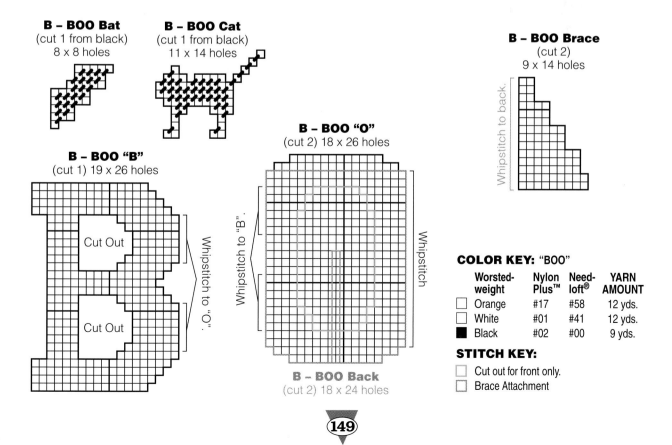

B – BOO Bat
(cut 1 from black)
8 x 8 holes

B – BOO Cat
(cut 1 from black)
11 x 14 holes

B – BOO Brace
(cut 2)
9 x 14 holes

Whipstitch to back.

B – BOO "B"
(cut 1) 19 x 26 holes

Cut Out

Cut Out

Whipstitch to "O".

Whipstitch to "B".

B – BOO "O"
(cut 2) 18 x 26 holes

Whipstitch

B – BOO Back
(cut 2) 18 x 24 holes

COLOR KEY: "BOO"

Worsted-weight	Nylon Plus™	Need-loft®	YARN AMOUNT
☐ Orange	#17	#58	12 yds.
☐ White	#01	#41	12 yds.
■ Black	#02	#00	9 yds.

STITCH KEY:
☐ Cut out for front only.
☐ Brace Attachment

Photo Hellos

PHOTO ON PAGE 148

A – LOVE "L"
(cut 1)
18 x 29 holes

Whipstitch to "O".

A – LOVE "O"
(cut 1) 21 x 29 holes

Whipstitch to "V".

Whipstitch to "L".

A – Love Back
(cut 1) 21 x 24 holes

A – LOVE "V"
(cut 1)
23 x 29 holes

Whipstitch to "O".

Whipstitch to "E".

A – LOVE "E"
(cut 1) 18 x 29 holes

Whipstitch to "V".

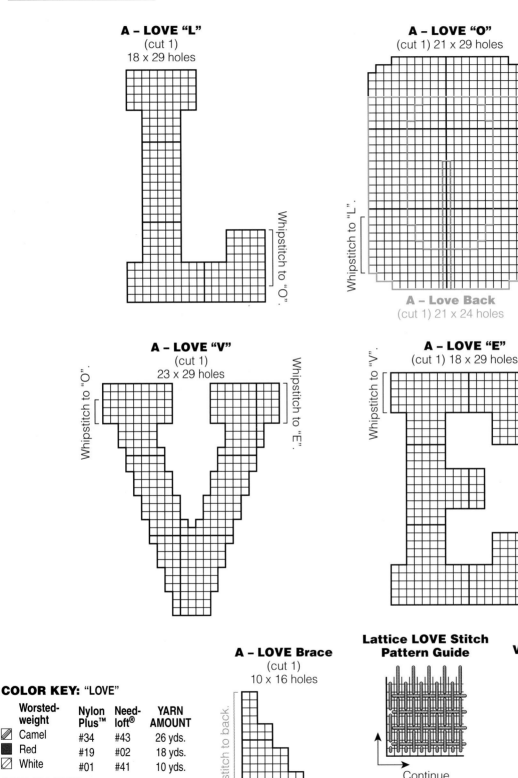

A – LOVE Brace
(cut 1)
10 x 16 holes

Whipstitch to back.

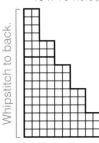

Lattice LOVE Stitch Pattern Guide

Continue established pattern up and across each entire piece.

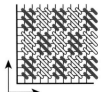

Valentine LOVE Stitch Pattern Guide

Continue established pattern up and across each entire piece.

COLOR KEY: "LOVE"

Worsted-weight	Nylon Plus™	Need-loft®	YARN AMOUNT
Camel	#34	#43	26 yds.
Red	#19	#02	18 yds.
White	#01	#41	10 yds.

STITCH KEY:

- Cut out for front only.
- Brace Attachment

Holiday Tissue Cover

Designed by Nancy W. Dorman

Add holiday spirit to any room when you stitch this collection of quick-change motifs.

Instructions on next page

Holiday Tissue Cover

PHOTO ON PAGE 151

SIZE: Snugly covers a boutique-style tissue box.

MATERIALS: Four sheets of 7-count plastic canvas; ⅔ yd. of Velcro® closure strip; Sewing needle and white thread (optional); Craft glue or glue gun; Six-strand embroidery floss (for amount see Color Key); Medium metallic braid or metallic ribbon (for amount see Color Key); Worsted-weight or plastic canvas yarn (for amounts see Color Key).

CUTTING INSTRUCTIONS:

A: For top, cut one according to graph.

B: For sides, cut four 29 x 37 holes (no graph).

C: For hearts, cut four according to graph.

D: For shamrocks, cut four according to graph.

E: For eggs, cut four according to graph.

F: For flowers, cut twelve according to graph.

G: For pumpkins, cut four according to graph.

H: For cornucopias, cut four according to graph.

I: For trees, cut four according to graph.

STITCHING INSTRUCTIONS:

1: Using colors and stitches indicated, work A and C-I pieces according to graphs; fill in uncoded area of E using white and Continental Stitch. Work B pieces using eggshell and pattern established on A. With matching colors as shown in photo, Overcast edges of C-I pieces.

2: Using six strands floss, braid or ribbon and yarn in colors indicated, Backstitch, Straight Stitch and French Knot, embroider detail on A-C, E, F, H and I pieces as indicated on graphs.

3: Using eggshell and Herringbone Overcast, Overcast cutout edges of A. Using eggshell and Herringbone Whipstitch, Whipstitch A and B pieces together, forming Cover; using Herringbone Overcast, Overcast unfinished edges.

NOTES: Cut Velcro® closure into twenty-four 1" pieces. Cut four 9" lengths of white.

4: Tie each 9" strand into a bow; trim ends. Glue one bow to each heart and three F pieces to each E as shown. Glue or sew one 1" piece of loopy-sided Velcro® to center of each Cover side; glue or sew one 1" piece of fuzzy-sided Velcro® to back of each motif.✧

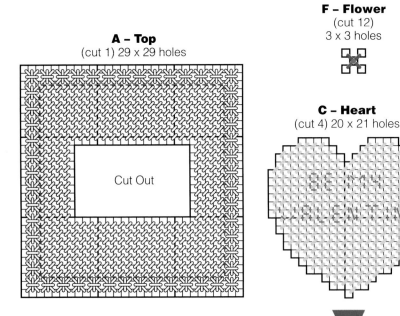

A – Top
(cut 1) 29 x 29 holes

Cut Out

F – Flower
(cut 12)
3 x 3 holes

C – Heart
(cut 4) 20 x 21 holes

COLOR KEY: Holiday Tissue Cover

Embroidery floss			AMOUNT
Dk. Green			½ yd.

Med. metallic braid or ribbon			AMOUNT
Gold			2 yds.

Worsted-weight	Nylon Plus™	Need-loft®	YARN AMOUNT
Eggshell	#24	#39	2½ oz.
Dk. Green	#31	#27	8 yds.
Red	#19	#02	7½ yds.
Dk. Orange	#18	#52	6 yds.
Lavender	#22	#45	4½ yds.
Cinnamon	#44	#14	3½ yds.
White	#01	#41	3 yds.
Black	#02	#00	1 yd.
Dk. Brown	#36	#15	1 yd.
Fern	#57	#23	1 yd.
Pink	#11	#07	1 yd.
Purple	#21	#46	1 yd.
Gold	#27	#17	½ yd.

STITCH KEY:

— Backstitch/Straight Stitch

● French Knot

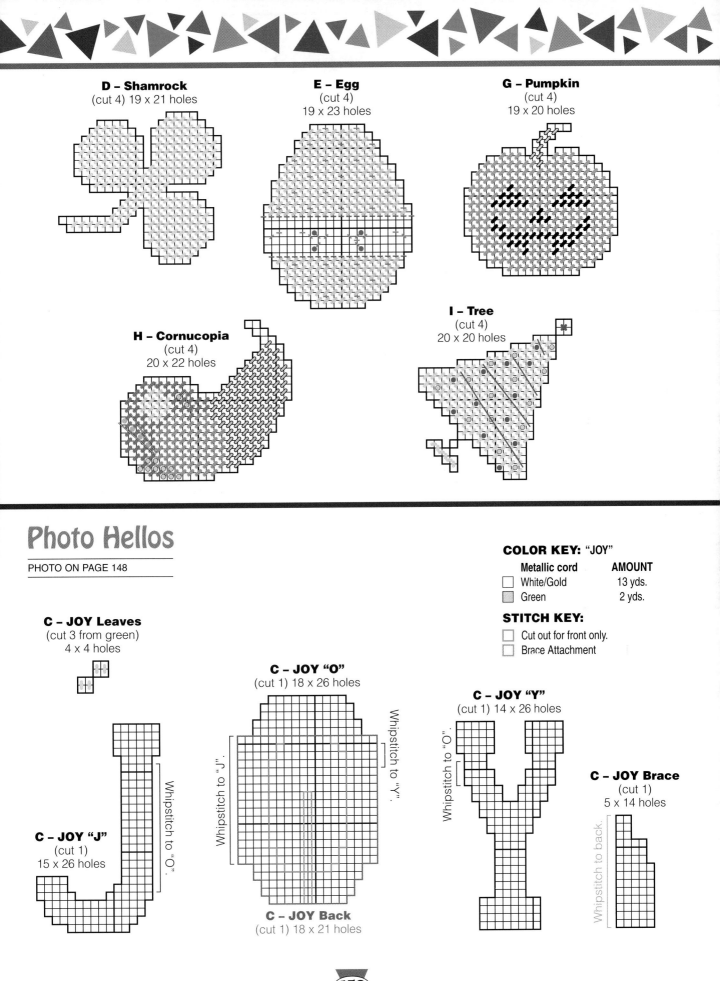

D – Shamrock
(cut 4) 19 x 21 holes

E – Egg
(cut 4)
19 x 23 holes

G – Pumpkin
(cut 4)
19 x 20 holes

H – Cornucopia
(cut 4)
20 x 22 holes

I – Tree
(cut 4)
20 x 20 holes

Photo Hellos

PHOTO ON PAGE 148

COLOR KEY: "JOY"

Metallic cord	AMOUNT
☐ White/Gold	13 yds.
▦ Green	2 yds.

STITCH KEY:

☐ Cut out for front only.
▢ Brace Attachment

C – JOY Leaves
(cut 3 from green)
4 x 4 holes

C – JOY "O"
(cut 1) 18 x 26 holes

Whipstitch to "J".

Whipstitch to "Y".

C – JOY "Y"
(cut 1) 14 x 26 holes

Whipstitch to "O".

C – JOY Brace
(cut 1)
5 x 14 holes

Whipstitch to back.

C – JOY "J"
(cut 1)
15 x 26 holes

Whipstitch to "O".

C – JOY Back
(cut 1) 18 x 21 holes

Ready, Set, Stitch!

Basic Instructions to Get You Started

Most plastic canvas stitchers love getting their projects organized before they even step out the door in search of supplies. A few moments of careful planning can make the creation of your project even more fun.

First of all, prepare your work area. You will need a flat surface for cutting and assembly, and you will need a place to store your materials. Good lighting is essential, and a comfortable chair will make your stitching time even more enjoyable.

Do you plan to make one project, or will you be making several of the same item? A materials list appears at the beginning of each pattern. If you plan to make several of the same item, multiply your materials accordingly. Your shopping list is ready.

Canvas

Most projects can be made using standard-size sheets of canvas. Standard-size sheets of 7-count (7 holes per inch) are always 70 x 90 holes and are about 10½" x 13½". For larger projects, 7-count canvas also comes in 12" x 18" (80 x 120 holes) and 13½" x 22½" (90 x 150 holes) sheets. Other shapes are available in 7-count, including circles, diamonds, purse forms and ovals.

10-count canvas (10 holes per inch) comes only in standard-size sheets, which vary slightly depending on brand. They are 10½" x 13½" (106 x 136 holes) or 11" x 14" (108 x 138 holes).

5-count canvas (5 holes per inch) and 14-count (14 holes per inch) sheets are also available.

Some canvas is soft and pliable, while other canvas is stiffer and more rigid. To prevent canvas from cracking during or after stitching, you'll want to choose pliable canvas for projects that require shaping, like round baskets with curved handles. For easier shaping, warm canvas pieces with a blow-dry hair dryer to soften; dip in cool water to set. If your project is a box or an item that will stand alone, stiffer canvas is more suitable.

Both 7- and 10-count canvas sheets are available in a rainbow of colors. Most designs can be stitched on colored as well as clear canvas. When a pattern does not specify color in the materials list, you can assume clear canvas was used in the photographed model. If you'd like to stitch only a portion of the design, leaving a portion unstitched, use colored canvas to coordinate with yarn colors.

Buy the same brand of canvas for each entire project. Different brands of canvas may differ slightly in the distance between each bar.

Marking & Counting Tools

To avoid wasting canvas, careful cutting of each piece is important. For some pieces with square corners, you might be comfortable cutting the canvas without marking it beforehand. But for pieces with lots of angles and cutouts, you may want to mark your canvas before cutting.

Always count before you mark and cut. To count holes on the graphs, look for the bolder lines showing each ten holes. These ten-count lines begin in the lower left-hand corner of each graph and are on the graph to make counting easier. To count holes on the canvas, you may use your tapestry needle, a toothpick or a plastic hair roller pick. Insert the needle or pick slightly in each hole as you count.

Most stitchers have tried a variety of marking tools and have settled on a favorite, which may be crayon, permanent marker, grease pencil or ball point pen. One of the best marking tools is a fine-point overhead projection marker, available at office supply stores. The ink is dark and easy to see and washes off completely with water. After cutting and before stitching, it's important to remove all marks so they won't stain yarn as you stitch or show through stitches later. Cloth and paper toweling removes grease pencil and crayon marks, as do fabric softener sheets that have already been used in your dryer.

Supplies

Yarn, canvas, needles, cutters and most other supplies needed to complete the projects in this book are available at craft and needlework stores and through mail order catalogs. Other supplies are available at fabric, hardware and discount stores. For mail order information, see page 159.

154

Cutting Tools

You may find it very helpful to have several tools on hand for cutting canvas. When cutting long, straight sections, scissors, craft cutters or kitchen shears are the fastest and easiest to use.

For cutting out detailed areas and trimming nubs, you may like using manicure scissors or nail clippers. Many stitchers love using Ultimate Plastic Canvas Cutters, available only from *The Needlecraft Shop* catalog. If you prefer laying your canvas flat when cutting, try a craft knife and cutting surface – self-healing mats designed for sewing and kitchen cutting boards work well.

Yarn and Other Stitching Materials

You may choose two-ply nylon plastic canvas yarn (the color numbers of two popular brands are found in the general materials lists and Color Keys) or four-ply worsted-weight yarn for stitching on 7-count canvas. There are about 42 yards per ounce of plastic canvas yarn and 50 yards per ounce of worsted-weight yarn.

Worsted-weight yarn is widely available and comes in wool, acrylic, cotton and blends. If you decide to use worsted-weight yarn, choose 100% acrylic for best coverage. Select worsted-weight yarn by color instead of the color names or numbers found in the Color Keys. Projects stitched with worsted-weight yarn often "fuzz" after use. "Fuzz" can be removed by shaving it off with a fabric shaver to make your project look new again.

Plastic canvas yarn comes in about 60 colors and is a favorite of many plastic canvas designers. These yarns "wear" well both while stitching and in the finished product. When buying plastic canvas yarn, shop using the color names or numbers found in the Color Keys, or select colors of your choice.

To cover 5-count canvas, use a doubled strand of worsted-weight or plastic canvas yarn.

Choose sport-weight yarn or #3 pearl cotton for stitching on 10-count canvas. To cover 10-count canvas using six-strand embroidery floss, use 12 strands held together. Single and double plies of yarn will also cover 10-count and can be used for embroidery or accent stitching worked over needlepoint stitches – simply separate worsted-weight yarn into 2-ply or plastic canvas yarn into 1-ply. Nylon plastic canvas yarn does not perform as well as knitting worsted when separated and

can be frustrating to use, but it is possible. Just use short lengths, separate into single plies and twist each ply slightly.

Embroidery floss or #5 pearl cotton can also be used for embroidery, and each covers 14-count canvas well.

Metallic cord is a tightly-woven cord that comes in dozens of glittering colors. Some are solid-color metallics, including gold and silver, and some have colors interwoven with gold or silver threads. If your metallic cord has a white core, the core may be removed for super-easy stitching. To do so, cut a length of cord; grasp center core fibers with tweezers or fingertips and pull. Core slips out easily. Though the sparkly look of metallics will add much to your project, you may substitute contrasting colors of yarn.

Natural and synthetic raffia straw will cover 7-count canvas if flattened before stitching. Use short lengths to prevent splitting, and glue ends to prevent unraveling.

Cutting Canvas

Follow all Cutting Instructions, Notes and labels above graphs to cut canvas. Each piece is labeled with a letter of the alphabet. Square-sided pieces are cut according to hole count, and some may not have a graph.

Unlike sewing patterns, graphs are not designed to be used as actual patterns but rather as counting, cutting and stitching guides. Therefore, graphs may not be actual size. Count the holes on the graph (see Marking & Counting Tools on page 154), mark your canvas to match, then cut. The old carpenters' adage – "Measure twice, cut once" – is good advice. Trim off the nubs close to the bar, and trim all corners diagonally.

For large projects, as you cut each piece, it is a good idea to label it with its letter and name. Use sticky labels, or fasten scrap paper notes through the canvas with a twist tie or a quick stitch with a scrap of yarn. To stay organized, you many want to store corresponding pieces together in zip-close bags.

If you want to make several of a favorite design to give as gifts or sell at bazaars, make cutting canvas easier and faster by making a master pattern. From colored canvas, cut out one of each piece required. For duplicates, place the colored canvas on top of clear canvas and cut out. If needed, secure the canvas pieces together with paper fasteners, twist ties or yarn. By using this method, you only have to count from the graphs once.

If you accidentally cut or tear a bar or two on your canvas, don't worry! Boo-boos can usually be repaired in one of several ways: heat the tip of a metal skewer and melt the canvas back together; glue torn bars with a tiny drop of craft glue, super glue or hot glue; or reinforce the torn section with a separate piece of canvas placed at the back of your work. When reinforcing with extra canvas, stitch through both thicknesses.

Needles & Other Stitching Tools

Blunt-end tapestry needles are used for stitching plastic canvas. Choose a No. 16 needle for stitching 5- and 7-count, a No. 18 for stitching 10-count and a No. 24 for stitching 14-count canvas. A small pair of embroidery scissors for snipping yarn is handy. Try using needle-nosed jewelry pliers for pulling the needle through several thicknesses of canvas and out of tight spots too small for your hand.

Stitching the Canvas

Stitching Instructions for each section are found after the Cutting Instructions. First, refer to the illustrations of basic stitches found on page 157 to familiarize yourself with the stitches used. Illustrations will be found near the graphs for pieces worked using special stitches. Follow the numbers on the tiny graph beside the illustration to make each stitch – bring your needle up from the back of the work on odd numbers and down through the front of the work on the even numbers.

Before beginning, read the Stitching Instructions to get an overview of what you'll be doing. You'll find that some pieces are stitched using colors and stitches indicated on graphs, and for other pieces you will be given a color and stitch to use to cover the entire piece.

Cut yarn lengths no longer than 18" to prevent fraying. Thread needle; do not tie a knot in the end. Bring your needle up through the canvas from the back, leaving a short length of yarn on the wrong side of the canvas. As you begin to stitch, work over this short length of yarn. If you are beginning with Continental Stitches, leave a 1" length, but if you are working longer stitches, leave a longer length.

In order for graph colors to contrast well, graph colors may not match yarn colors. For instance, a light yellow may be selected to represent the metallic cord color gold, or a light blue may represent white yarn.

When following a graph showing several colors, you may want to work all the stitches of one color at the same time. Some stitchers prefer to work with several colors at once by threading each on a separate needle and letting the yarn not being used hang on the wrong side of the work. Either way, remember that strands of yarn run across the wrong side of the work may show through the stitches from the front.

As you stitch, try to maintain an even tension on the yarn. Loose stitches will look uneven, and tight stitches will let the canvas show through. If your yarn twists as you work, you may want to let your needle and yarn hang and untwist occasionally.

When you end a section of stitching or finish a thread, weave the yarn through the back side of your last few stitches, then trim it off.

Construction & Assembly

After all pieces of an item needing assembly are stitched, you will find the order of assembly is listed in the Stitching Instructions and sometimes illustrated in Diagrams found with the graphs. For best results, join pieces in the order written. Refer to the Stitch Key and to the directives near the graphs for precise attachments.

Finishing Tips

To combat glue strings when using a hot glue gun, practice a swirling motion as you work. After placing the drop of glue on your work, lift the gun slightly and swirl to break the stream of glue, as if you were making an ice cream cone. Have a cup of water handy when gluing. For those times that you'll need to touch the glue, first dip your finger into the water just enough to dampen it. This will minimize the glue sticking to your finger, and it will cool and set the glue more quickly.

To attach beads, use a bit more glue to form a cup around the bead. If too much shows after drying, use a craft knife to trim off excess glue.

Scotchguard® or other fabric protectors may be used on your finished projects. However, avoid using a permanent marker if you plan to use a fabric protector, and be sure to remove all other markings before stitching. Fabric protectors can cause markings to bleed, staining yarn.

For More Information

Sometimes even the most experienced needlecrafters can find themselves having trouble following instructions. If you have difficulty completing your project, write to Plastic Canvas Editors, *The Needlecraft Shop*, 23 Old Pecan Road, Big Sandy, Texas 75755.

Stitch Guide

CONTINENTAL STITCH

can be used to stitch designs or fill in background areas.

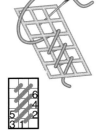

OVERCAST

is used to finish edges. Stitch two or three times in corners for complete coverage.

LONG STITCH

is a horizontal or vertical stitch used to stitch designs or fill in background areas. Can be stitched over two or more bars.

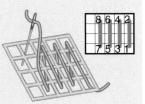

SLANTED GOBELIN STITCH

can be used to stitch designs or fill in background areas. Can be stitched over two or more bars in vertical or horizontal rows.

LOOPED OVERCAST

CROSS STITCH

can be used as a needlepoint stitch or as an embroidery stitch stitched over background stitches with contrasting yarn or floss.

HERRINGBONE OVERCAST

WHIPSTITCH

is used to join two or more pieces together.

MODIFIED TURKEY WORK STITCH

is used to fill in background areas or as an embroidery stitch to add a loopy or fringed texture. Stitch over one bar leaving a loop, then stitch over the same bar to anchor the loop.

RYA KNOT STITCH

is used to fill in background areas or as an embroidery stitch to add a loopy or fringed texture. Stitch over two bars leaving a loop, then stitch over the next two bars to anchor the loop.

HERRINGBONE WHIPSTITCH

EMBROIDERY STITCHES

BACKSTITCH

is usually used as an embroidery stitch to outline or add detail. Stitches can be any length and go in any direction.

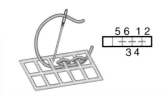

LARK'S HEAD KNOT

FRENCH KNOT

is usually used as an embroidery stitch to add detail. Can be made in one hole or over a bar. If dot on graph is in hole as shown, come up and go down with needle in same hole.

LAZY DAISY STITCH

is usually used as an embroidery stitch to add detail. Can be any length and go in any direction. Come up and go down in same hole, leaving loop. Come up in another hole for top of stitch, put needle through loop and go down in same hole.

FLY STITCH

is usually used as an embroidery stitch to add detail. Curve Straight Stitch and anchor at center with one small stitch in hole or over bar.

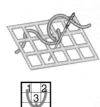

RUNNING STITCH

is used as a straight line stitch to add detail. Stitches can be any length and go in any direction.

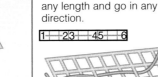

STRAIGHT STITCH

is usually used as an embroidery stitch to add detail. Stitches can be any length and can go in any direction. Looks like Backstitch except stitches do not touch.

SMYRNA CROSS STITCH

can be used as a needlepoint stitch or as an embroidery stitch stitched over background stitches with contrasting yarn or floss.

Acknowledgments

We would like to express our appreciation to the many people who helped create this book. Our special thanks go to each of the talented designers who contributed original designs. Special thanks, also, to Santee Print Works and V.I.P. Fabrics for allowing us to photograph and reproduce their fabric designs for the divider pages in this book.

Finally, we wish to express our gratitude to the following manufacturers for their generous contribution of materials and supplies:

Darice®:

Nylon Plus™ yarn – *Jolly Snowmen, July 4th Picnic, Shamrock Welcome*

Canvas – *Jolly Snowmen, Rudolph's Magic, Old World Santas, North Star Nativity, God's Promise, Biblical Accents, Midnight Mobile, Cone Ornaments, Time to Celebrate*

Metallic cord – *Santa's Elves, Christmas Stocking, Happy Christmas, Glittery Centerpiece, Angels Around the World, Festive Table Decor, Shamrock Welcome, Cottontail Cuties, Midnight Mobile*

Music button – *Rudolph's Magic,*
Gemstones – *Glittery Centerpiece*
Raffia straw – *Shamrock Welcome*

DMC:

Embroidery floss – *Jolly Snowmen, Dazzling Trio, Cottontail Cuties*
#3 pearl cotton – *Santa Hanger, Happy Christmas, Frosty Box, Seasonal Welcome*

Uniek® Crafts:

Needloft® yarn – *Santa's Elves, Christmas Stocking, Santa Hanger, Happy Christmas, Frosty Box, Dazzling Trio, North Star Nativity, Angels Around the World, Holiday Gift Bag, Valentine Bags, Festive Table Decor, Cottontail Cuties, Bright 'n' Bold, God's Promise, Cone Ornaments, Time to Celebrate, Seasonal Welcome*

Canvas – *Dazzling Trio, Glittery Centerpiece, Valentine Bags, Festive Table Decor, Bright 'n' Bold*
Metallic cord – *Dazzling Trio, Time to Celebrate*

Kreinik:

Metallic braid – *Christmas Stocking, Old World Santas, Biblical Accents*
Metallic ribbon – *Dazzling Trio, Biblical Accents*

Creative Beginnings:
Charms – *Old World Santas*

Aleene's™:
Designer Tacky Glue – *Glittery Centerpiece, Cone Ornaments*

Coats & Clark:
Anchor® embroidery floss – *Cone Ornaments*
J. & P. Coats® plastic canvas yarn – *Jack-o-Lantern Box*
J. & P. Coats® embroidery floss – *Angels Around the World, Biblical Accents*

Wright's®:
Ribbon – *Cone Ornaments*

Kunin/Foss Mfg:
Presto Felt™ – *Cone Ornaments*

Walnut Hollow Farm, Inc.:
Clock movement – *Time to Celebrate*

Index